Berol.

POCKET GUIDE TO

Calligraphy

Susanne Haines studied calligraphy and bookbinding at Stuart Digby College, Roehampton Institute. She has taught calligraphy at adult education classes for many years and is a visiting tutor on the lettering course at the City and Guilds of London Art School. Susanne also works as a freelance calligrapher and editor and is the author of The Calligrapher's Project Book *(Collins, 1987).*

Berol.

POCKET GUIDE TO

Calligraphy

Susanne Haines

With thanks to Jo for the ant, bat, cat and duck, and the delight.

Published exclusively for Berol Limited
Oldmedow Road, King's Lynn, Norfolk PE30 4JR.

by Design Eye Limited
8 Fouberts Place, London W1V 1HH

ISBN 1 872700 00 4

SECOND IMPRESSION
Printed in England

The author and publishers would like to thank Anness Law Limited for their editorial assistance on this project.

CONTENTS

All the writing in the book was done with Berol fibre pens, and so all the references to nib sizes refer to these pens. The work was reduced for reproduction.

INTRODUCTION

Calligraphy is the art of beautiful writing. Letters are written with a broad-edged pen to give the characteristic strokes with their strongly contrasting thick and thin lines.

Calligraphy gives letters and words a personal voice and an image – it is sensual writing. Our eyes, so accustomed to the mechanical correctness of the printed word, and often offended by slapdash, functional lettering find relief and delight in their forms. Our hands, so used to scribbling notes, essays or memos in the quickest possible time in careless handwriting or on word-processors, can enjoy the careful considered formation of pleasing shapes and designs. Our minds, so full of important and trivial matters, can be given time to revel in the indulgence of concentrating on something that brings personal pleasure.

This pocket book introduces you to one of the most convenient calligraphic tools – the fibre tipped pen, takes you through the steps to understanding how to use it, demonstrates some of the alphabets that you can use and points out the basic design principles that you need to know. It then gives you a wealth of ideas on how to put your new-found skill into practice in specially designed projects, and, in most of them there is just a touch of light-heartedness.

To acquire a 'good hand' you will need a great deal of patience and practice. Unless you are exceptionally gifted, or lucky, the letters, unfortunately, will not flow perfectly as if by magic from the pen until you have studied quite hard. However, do allow yourself freedom to enjoy them, let your letters dance on the page, and remember that the idiosyncrasies of hand-written letter forms are all part of what gives them their charm.

Below are given the terms that are used in the book in relation to parts of the letter.

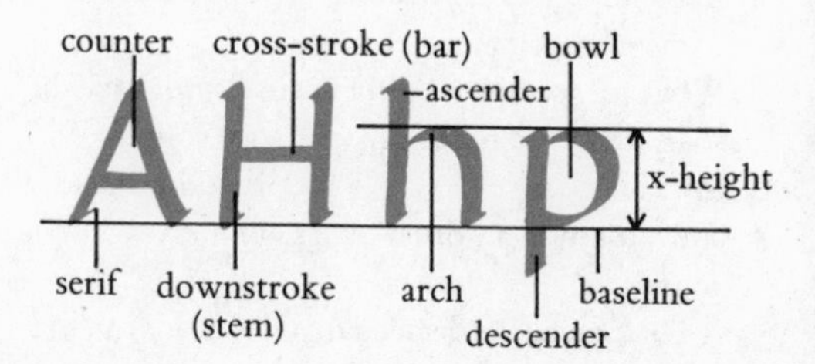

MATERIALS AND EQUIPMENT

You will need very little to make a start with calligraphy. A fibre pen and some paper are the bare essentials if you just want to try it out. However, once you have become addicted to this fascinating craft, you are sure to build up quite a collection of materials and equipment.

Traditionally, the reed pen and the quill were used in the writing of manuscripts. Today these tools are still used, but more popular is the steel dip pen (and, for handwriting, fountain pens). In recent years fibre pens have given calligraphers a very welcome new breed of pen to use. Professionals and beginners alike can enjoy the freedom of writing that they give and the convenience of having a ready supply of ink. While for some work, fibre pens do not have the sharpness required to give the crisp contrast of thick and thin strokes, particularly on a small scale, for more informal work and for working roughs they are ideal.

Once you have decided that you want to

pursue this craft you should equip yourself with the following basic essentials:

Pens: fibre pen, fountain pen or dip pen with a reservoir to hold the ink supply. (Remember to take care of your pens to give them a longer life. Close the lids of fibre pens tightly shut after use, and clean ink off dip pens and store them dry to prevent rusting.)

Ink: Fountain pen ink for fountain pens, non-waterproof ink for dip pens. Not necessary for fibre pens.

Paper: Layout paper is good for practice (for fibre pens use layout paper specially made for use with marker pens which gives a crisper line); cartridge paper (with a smooth surface for fibre pens) is also useful. There is a vast selection available – pay a visit to a specialist shop and ask for advice.

Ruler, pencil and **eraser.**

Drawing board: This can be made cheaply from a piece of thick hardboard, chipboard or blockboard; cover it with a few layers of paper, held on with tape, to soften the surface slightly.

Lastly, you will need a table and good light.

USING THE EDGED PEN

By following the steps on the next few pages you will discover how to make your broad-edged pen work for you, and then when you have understood this, you can go on to study the alphabets that follow.

But first, explore for yourself without any guidance, the marks that the pen will make, drawing curves and lines, trying out some letters, and holding the pen so that the broad edge of the nib is at different angles on the paper.

Now prepare to make sense of what is going on. First, make sure you are sitting comfortably, prop up your drawing board at an angle (rest it on a pencil box or tin), arrange your paper (ideally A3 size layout paper) squarely on the board and draw some horizontal pencil lines about 1 inch (2.5cm) apart and use a wide fibre pen about ⅛ inch (3mm) wide.

Hold the pen lightly in your hand, and ensure that the strokes you make use the whole broad edge of the nib.

Hold the pen with the nib at 0° (ie flat) to the writing line and make some downward strokes. Now make some strokes with the pen nib held at 90° (ie vertical) to the writing line. These are the thickest and thinnest lines the pen will make.

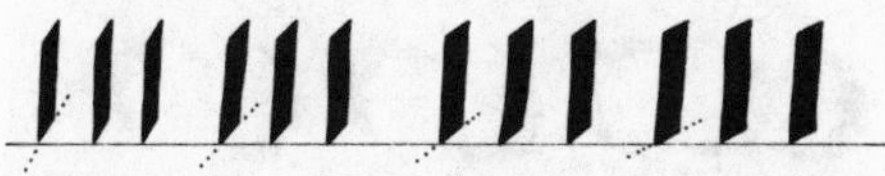

Make a series of pen strokes at a variety of angles, from steep to shallow. An angle of 45° should feel natural and comfortable.

These pen strokes are written at 45° – the angle used for italic and gothic. The vertical and horizontal strokes are of equal width.

If the pen nib is held at an angle of 30°, the down strokes are thicker than the cross strokes. This is the correct angle for roundhand.

Write some anti-clockwise and clockwise curves with the pen at 0°, always starting at the thinnest part of the curve at the top. Try curves at 90° – you'll find this rather awkward.

Write a series of curves at different angles.

Join up the anti-clockwise and clockwise curves at the thin part to make a circle. Write the anti-clockwise curve first. Don't push the pen up around the right side – there should be no joins in the thick part of the stems.

Write a series of diagonal strokes at different angles, always working from top to bottom.

ORDER OF STROKES

Write a square, circle and triangle following the order of strokes shown (the horizontal stroke of the triangle can be written second or third), then write the simple capitals based on these forms.

When you are using the edged pen for writing letter forms always pull the pen towards you, don't push against the broad edge. Work from top to bottom and left to right. (NB It is possible to push fibre tip pens, although the lines will be slightly less precise. Fibre tip pens are particularly useful for rapid writing.)

You can push the pen when making a diagonal stroke with the thin edge; it can be pushed or pulled as there is no resistance from the broad edge. This is necessary for italics.

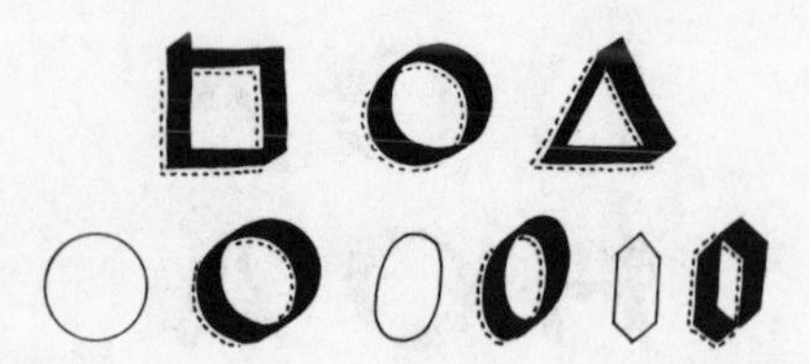

BASIC FORM

The edged pen adds weight to an underlying structure (see square, circle and triangle). The most important basic form of letters is generally the letter 'o'. The examples shown above relate to the alphabets given further on in this book: the circular 'o' for roundhand, an oval 'o' for italic and the angular 'o' for gothic.

All the letters of an alphabet should relate to one another harmoniously and appear to belong to the same family. It is best to learn each alphabet in groups of similarly constructed letters.

PEN ANGLE

Basic form is affected by pen angle. Draw a series of squares with changing pen angles and notice how the basic form of the square changes because of the different positions of the thick and thin strokes. The counter space has clearly been turned through 90° between the first and last of the squares shown.

LETTER WEIGHT

Basic form is also affected by the weight of the letter (ie the ratio of stem area to the letter size). The height of the letter is not measured with a ruler, but in terms of nib-widths (ie how many times the height of the letter can be divided by the full width of the pen). Draw squares at a height of 4, 2, 5 and 6 nib-widths.

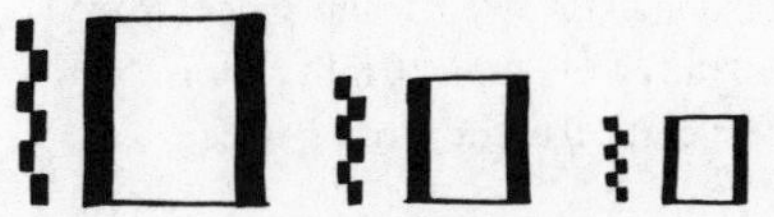

Of course, the height measured in nib-widths relates to the nib-width of the pen you are using.

Draw a sequence of squares with pens of different sizes at a height of 6 nib-widths.

ROUNDHAND

This is an ideal small letter alphabet to learn as a beginner because its shapes are simple, bold and round, and because the letters are based on a circular 'O', a much more reliable basic geometric shape than an oval. Take as much notice of the space created inside the letters as the strokes themselves.

Use the guidelines given for writing the alphabet shown here. Once you have mastered it you may want to make some changes and start to add your personality to the letters.

The key letter form is a circular 'o'. The height of the 'o' (or x-height) is 4 nib-widths; the ascenders and descenders are about 6 nib-widths. The pen angle for the strokes (except some diagonals) is 30°. The line space (space between the baselines) is 10 nib-widths. Stems should be vertical to the writing line.

Opposite: follow the order of strokes and change the pen angle where dotted lines are shown (further explanation is given on the next pages).

abcde

fghijk

lmnop

qrstuv

wxyz

LEARNING ROUNDHAND

Use a wide pen to practise the alphabet so that you get the maximum contrast of thick and thin and so that you can see clearly what you are doing. Rule up a sheet of paper with the baselines 10 nib-widths apart to allow for a space between the ascenders and descenders of letters on consecutive lines. Follow the order shown here:

Start with some straight vertical lines, leading in and out of each stroke with a tiny fine stroke along the thin edge of the pen. Practise some simple curves – left and right halves of a circle.

Superimpose an 'n' on top of an 'o'. The curve of the 'n' follows the top of the curve of the 'o'. The curved stroke of the 'n' starts from inside the straight stem. These two letters form the basis for two letter groups – round ('o', 'c', 'd', 'g', 'q', 'b', 'p') and arched ('n', 'm', 'h', 'r', 'a', 'y').

cdgqbp

Write the group of round letters (which are based on the curve of the 'o').

ccdgq

The top of the 'c' is slightly flattened. The 'd', 'g' and 'q' are built on the 'c'. [The tail of the 'g' should be a smooth curve.]

bp x p

Keep the curve of 'b' and 'p' very round, starting the stroke inside the vertical stem. Do not hook the bottom curve of the 'p' (the left edge of the pen should start on the baseline).

nmhray

This group of arched letters should all have generous curves, again with the curves forming a strong join. The 'u' and 'y' (shown superimposed) are based on an inverted 'n'.

ilt

The 'i' should have a slightly curved base, the 'l' and 't' have a more generous curve.

The cross-bars of 't' and 'f' should hang from the x-height line. This helps to keep a strong line along the top of the letters. The 't' is short; the 'f' starts with a curved stroke.

s s s o

The letter 's' should have a balanced serpentine curve. If you have difficulties with it, write it inside an 'o'. The top and bottom curves should be slightly flattened curves, not hooks.

x x v w y

The pen angle on letters with diagonal strokes should be altered in order to give an appearance of equal stroke width (see 'x'). Steepen the wide strokes on 'v', 'w' and 'x' to thin them down a little. Write the thinner stroke of the 'x' at a shallower angle to thicken it a little.

k z

The two diagonals of 'k' and the diagonal of 'z' are flattened a little for a more even distribution of weight.

Once you have begun to master the basic alphabet, you may want to introduce your own style by varying certain aspects of the design of individual letters.

g o g g g

This is an attractive alternative form of the 'g'. Keep the bowl smaller than the letter 'o'.

h n n n

one one

You can vary the height of the ascenders and descenders (7 nib–widths is a common height for an x–height of 4), but do not make them too tall or they will look ungainly. The x–height can also be varied. Letters tend to naturally be written narrower when they are tall, and they become wider when the letter is shorter.

You can also deliberately alter the basic form of the letter, for instance by narrowing the circular 'o' to an oval or by squaring the shape. Remember to make all the letters harmonize by changing them group by group.

The serifs (the finish given to the stems) can also be varied.

The fine curved lead-in lines can be accentuated. This is best done on the lead in and out of the letters, and avoided at the bottom of the first stroke of the 'n' (and similar strokes) to prevent a heavy look in the middle of the letter.

Serifs can, of course, be left off altogether, with a blunt end to the strokes.

Hairline serifs can be added to the stems with the thin edge of the pen.

Wedge serifs give a chunky look to stems. They are made with two strokes, the first is a small curve, the second is an upward hairline stroke followed by a downstroke.

ROUNDHAND CAPITALS

These capitals are based on a circular 'O' and used with roundhand small letters. It is important that they all relate to one another in terms of shape and proportion and look as if they belong together.

These capitals are very versatile: far from being used only for headings, or as initial capitals for roundhand, they can be written *en masse*, and in a variety of weights, sizes and spacing offer considerable scope for design.

Once you have understood them, you will find it easier to write other types of capitals: versals can be based on their forms, italics can be adapted from them, and even decorated gothic letters will pose fewer problems.

The key letter form is a circular 'O'. The height of the letters is 6 nib-widths. The pen angle for the strokes (except some diagonals) is 30°. Stems should be vertical to the writing line.

Opposite: follow the order of strokes shown and change the pen angle where dotted lines are shown (further explanation is given on the next pages).

ABCD
EFGHI
JKLM
NOPQ
RSTUV
WXYZ

LEARNING ROUNDHAND CAPITALS

Rule up a paper with lines at intervals of 6 nib-widths of a wide pen and write on every other line. The main letter 'groups' are: round, based on a circle ('O', 'C', 'D', 'G', 'Q'); narrower than the circle ('H', 'N', 'U', 'A', 'V', 'T', 'X', 'Y' and 'Z'); narrower still ('B', 'P', 'R', 'E', 'F', 'L', 'K', 'I', 'J' and 'S'); the same width as ('M') and wider than the circle ('W').

QCDG

Write an 'O' and a 'Q', and then the letters which use the same curves. The top curve of 'C' and 'G' is slightly flattened. The top of the curve of 'D' is quite straight.

HNU

These letters with vertical sides are narrower than the 'O'. The cross-bar of the 'H' should be above the midpoint to give it balance. Steepen the vertical strokes of the 'N' if they look heavy.

AVT
XYZ

These are the same width as the letters 'H', 'N' and 'U'. The cross-bar of the 'A' should be just below the midpoint. Steepen the pen angle of the wide strokes of 'A', 'V', 'X' and 'Y'. Flatten the pen angle for the thin strokes of 'V', 'X' and 'Y', and for the diagonal of 'Z'.

BPR

These letters are narrower than the previous group. The base of 'B' should be larger than the top. The bowls of 'P' and 'R' are larger than that of 'B'. Flatten the pen angle of the diagonal stroke of 'R'. The straightness at the top of the letters echoes the shape of the 'D'.
There is also a horizontal movement in the middle of the letters.

EFKLI

These are the same width as the previous group. The cross-bars of 'E' and 'F' should be slightly above the midpoint of the letter. The diagonals of 'K' should just touch the vertical stroke (to avoid heaviness at this point).

JS

Also of the same narrow width, these letters should have smooth curves. The 'S' is written in the same way as the small letter but it is narrower.

MW

The 'M' is the same width as the 'O'. Do not allow the outside strokes to slant too much, and keep a strong 'V'-shape in the centre. The first, second and fourth strokes should be steepened to thin the strokes a little.

ABCDEFGHIJ

KLMNOPQRSTU

ABCDEF

ABCDEFGHIJKLMNOP

ABCDEFGHIJKLMNOP

AAEEGGRR

A VARIETY OF CAPITALS

Top to bottom: narrow capitals 6 nib-widths high written with a fine pen and a medium pen; capitals 4 nib-widths high written with a wide pen and a medium pen; capitals 4 nib-widths high written with a fine pen with serifs added; variations on 'A', 'E', 'G' and 'R'.

VERSALS

These letters are based on the same proportions and shape as the roundhand capitals but they are more complicated to write as the wide stems are built up from a series of strokes made with a fine pen. The stems of the letters opposite are filled in, but you can leave them unfilled,

Use the guidelines given for writing these versals before making your own changes.

The key basic letter form is again the circular 'O'. The height of the letter is about 8 or 9 times the width of the wide stem. To make the wide stems use the pen at a shallow angle; for the thin stems use the pen turned at an angle that gives the full width of the nib (ie at 90° for a horizontal stroke); for the serifs turn the pen to give the thinnest stroke.

The method for constructing the stems is shown below. The order of writing the letters is similar to the roundhand capitals.

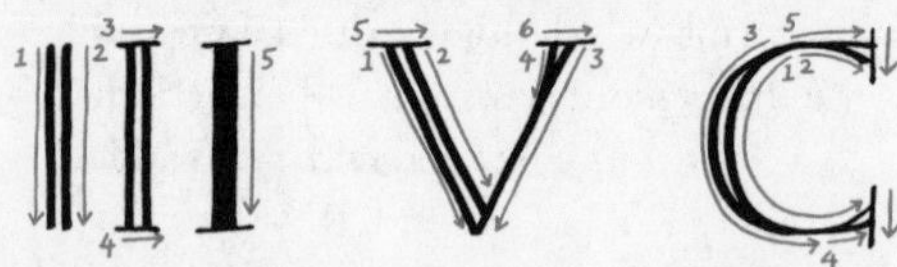

ABCD
EFGHI
JKLM
NOPQ
RSTUV
WXYZ

ITALIC

Italic is probably the most popular and the most useful of calligraphic alphabets. Once you have mastered it, you will find that you can develop quite a rhythm in your writing because of the springing nature of the strokes. The letters are narrow and sloped and the down strokes of the letters should all run parallel to each other.

Use the guidelines given for writing the alphabet before making your own changes.

The basic/key letter is an oval 'o'. The x-height is 5 nib-widths; ascenders and descenders are about 9 nib-widths. The pen angle for the strokes (except some diagonals) is 45°. Line space 13 nib-widths from baseline to baseline. Stems should slope about 5° or 10° to the right of the vertical.

The 'a' is a key letter in this alphabet

Opposite: follow the order of strokes for these letters shown and change the pen angle where dotted lines are shown.

abcdefg

hijklmn

opqrstu

vwxyz

LEARNING ITALICS

Use a wide nib to start with and rule up a sheet of paper to the measurements given. This allows for generous ascenders and descenders – you may wish to make them a little shorter. Practice the alphabet in the order given here to see the relation of forms.

oces

The oval 'o' forms the basis of 'e' and 'c'. Do not make the bowl of 'e' too large or it will appear to sag. Write 's' in this group to remind you to keep it narrow.

adgquy

The arches of this group of letters all take off in an anti-clockwise direction. The 'a' is a key letter of this alphabet, so it is important to get it right.

If you find it difficult, think of it as a triangle with curved lines. The first stroke sweeps right up to the top of the x-height (so here you will be breaking the rule of not pushing the pen).

nhmbpkr

The arches of these letters are written in a clockwise direction and should echo the shapes of the letters in the previous group. Check that you maintain consistency in the arches, curves and counter spaces.

vwxz

Alter the pen angle of these diagonal strokes in a similar way to roundhand letters. The 'w' is written in two strokes, pushing the pen up for the second stroke.

ITALIC FLOURISHES

Flourishes should look as if they grow from the letters. With felt pens they can be made in a single movement but with dip pens they are best broken down and restarted at their thinnest points. You may want to draw them first with a pencil as a guide.

abcdefghij abcdefghijklmn

Italic is successful in a variety of weights. The letters on the left and right are 7 and barely 3 nib-widths high and were drawn with fine and medium pens respectively.

ABCDEFG

HIJKLMN

OPQRSTU

VWXYZ

AENRW

Italic capitals are similarly constructed to round-hand capitals but they are narrower and sloped to match the small letters. These are 7 nib-widths high. Try some flourishes with them.

GOTHIC

This highly decorative and angular script has a very forceful character. Its strongly vertical form, its often extreme narrowness, and the fragmented stems all make it an alphabet whose chief quality is that of decoration rather than legibility.

When writing this alphabet aim for strong parallel vertical stems, even spaces inside the letters (about one nib-width), and good joins at the top and bottom of the stems.

Decorative gothic capitals are given over the page. You can also use large decorated versals with the small letters.

Use the guidelines given for writing the alphabet here before making your own changes.

The basic/key letter form is an angular 'o'. The x-height is 5 nib-widths; the ascenders and descenders are about 7 nib-widths. The pen angle for the strokes is 45°. The line space is 9 nib-widths. Stems should be vertical to the writing line.

Opposite: follow the order of strokes for the letters.

LEARNING GOTHIC

Use a wide pen and rule up the paper. To start with, you could rule an additional line about one nib-width inside the two lines as a guide for the change of angle at top and bottom. Notice the different endings to the stems as shown below.

Start the first stroke of these letters below the top of the x-height line to allow for strokes that will join at the top. The bases of 'o', 'g', 'q' and 's' are angular, those of 'c' and 'e' are curved.

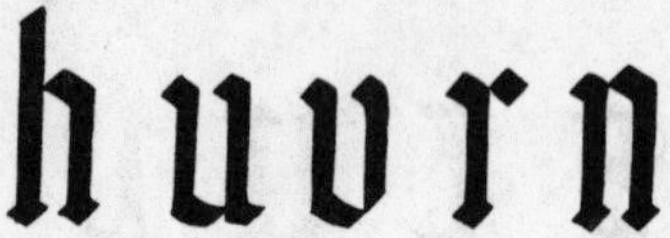

The 'h' has an abrupt start to its stem; the feet are made with separate pen strokes slightly offset from the stems. The rest of the letters here lead in with a small diagonal stroke, and differ in the way they are treated at the base of the letter.

A B C D E

F G H I J K

L M N O P

Q R S T U

V W X Y Z

These gothic capitals are written with a thinner pen than the small letters. Use roundhand capitals as a guide for the order of strokes. Add the hooks which are like curved full stops; the thin lines are added with the corner of a felt pen or the thin edge of a pen.

NUMBERS & PUNCTUATION

These numbers are for use with roundhand small letters and capitals and can be adapted for other scripts.

Written with a large pen, numbers should be kept at the same height as the small letters they are written with. When writing on a smaller scale they can be a little larger. 3, 4, 5, 7 and 9 go below the line, 6 and 8 slightly above.

1 2 3 4 5

6 7 8 9 0

May 15th

12345
67890

IN 1789

Numbers should be the same height as capitals.

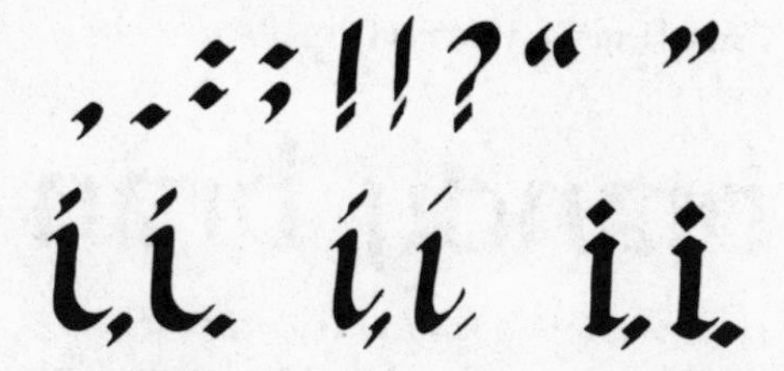

Punctuation should be kept discreet; for exclamation and question marks try using a smaller pen.

SPACING

The ability to space letters well depends initially on writing many well-shaped letters; you will gradually be able to judge what looks right. There are some guidelines to help you, but remember that the first two letters that you write determine your whole spacing system.

HONEY

The largest space should be between two straight-sided letters, and the spaces between all other letters should look visually equal to this (ie between a straight stem and a curve it is less). Capital letters are particularly effective when widely spaced.

brandy br×an

There should be a balance of space inside and outside the letters. Stand away from your work to judge the evenness. Some letters, such as 'r' and 'a', should be brought close together to avoid gaps in the words.

somemilk

Word-spacing depends on the letter-spacing: if letters are tightly spaced, words can be more tightly spaced too. In general you should allow enough space for an 'o' to just touch words on either side.

Warm some milk with a
little brandy and honey
and drink before bedtime
to ensure a sound sleep.

Line-spacing depends on letter- and word-spacing; in most cases it should be wider than the word space and allow room for ascenders and descenders.

Notice here that the two middle lines appear to be closer to each other because the ascenders and descenders fill up the space; in some cases measured accuracy in ruling lines has to be adjusted slightly by eye.

DESIGN & LAYOUT

Rather than writing and rewriting words until you are happy with the design, use the simple practical technique of cutting and pasting to help you reach your solution.

First write them out, concentrating on the writing and the spacing. Now cut out the words or lines according to the way you would like to rearrange them and glue them to a piece of paper, adjusting the spaces between the lines.

You can lead a horse to water

but you cannot make him

drink.

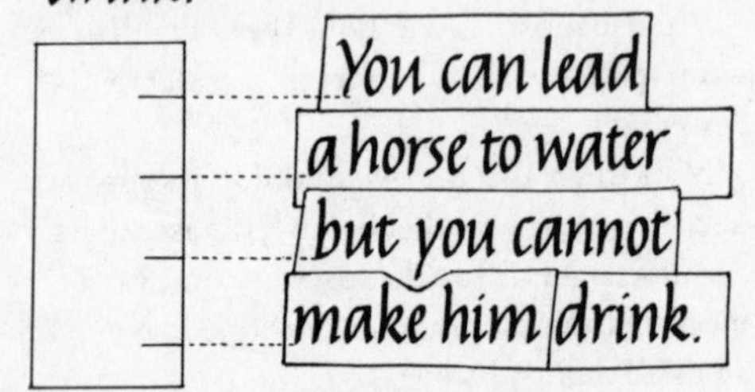

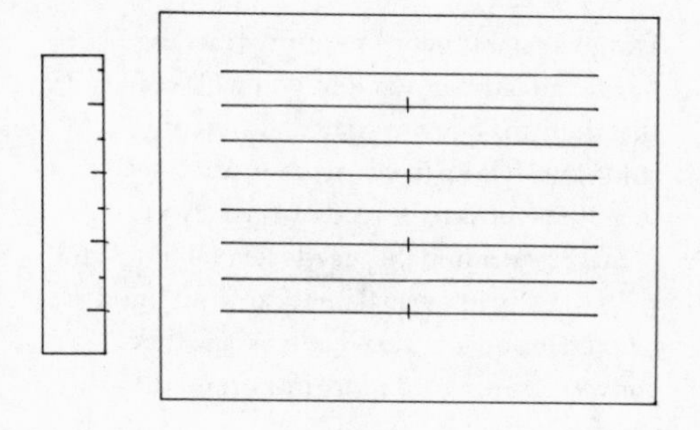

Since you pasted down the design by eye it is likely that the line spaces will vary, so you will need to take an average measurement and mark out another paper ruler. Transfer these marks lightly in pencil onto a good piece of paper and rule out, accurately, a baseline and a line for the top of the x-height (you may want to ignore the top line when you are confident in your writing). Write out the piece using the rough as a guide.

If you want to position the lines centrally on the paper, use the strips from your paste-up as a guide. Simply fold each line in half and match its central point to a centre line on the paper.

Designs can be made by simply rearranging the lines as already shown, but you will soon realize that there may be a myriad of different solutions. It is up to you to choose how you want the words to be read by the viewer.

Start by reading the words several times and see if they form a visual image in your mind, or evoke a mood; decide what message they convey. Is one word more important than another?

There are many ways of creating moods and giving emphasis to words, some of which are illustrated here.

The piece was simply written out (1) and then the last word was spaced out to fill the line, giving a horizontal format (2). These line breaks interrupt the phrases of the sentence (3), whereas these make more sense (4). Emphasis can be given to the most important word by increasing its weight, using a wider pen (5), by using capitals (6) or with colour (7). Two areas of emphasis can be treated differently (8). Capitals are very emphatic, and here they are spaced to occupy the same line length; the areas of colour are, however deliberately unbalanced (9).

1 If there's one thing I can't stand, it's
intolerance.

2 If there's one thing I can't stand, it's
I·N·T·O·L·E·R·A·N·C·E

3 If there's one
thing I can't
stand, it's
intolerance

4 If there's one thing
I can't stand,
it's intolerance

5 If there's one thing
I can't stand, it's
intolerance

6 If there's one thing
I can't stand, it's
INTOLERANCE.

7 If there's one thing
I can't stand, it's
INTOLERANCE

8 If there's
·ONE THING·
I can't stand, it's
INTOLERANCE

9 IF THERE'S ONE THING
I CAN'T STAND, IT'S
I N T O L E R A N C E

IF
THERE'S
ONE
THING
I
CAN'T
STAND,
IT'S
INTOLERANCE

How beautiful it is to do nothing
and then to sit down again afterwards
and rest

·:. SPANISH PROVERB :·

Top: in this design the words lead the eye down to the most important one. Above: the large initial, the flourish and the tiny capitals give contrast here.

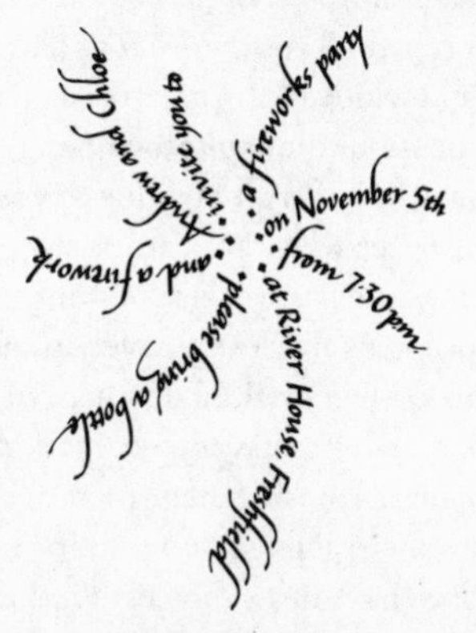

Top: text areas are balanced diagonally across the paper, linked by the drawing; colour lends emphasis to the name. Above: the curved radiating lines give interest and movement.

COPYING AND PRINTING

Photocopying is a good and inexpensive way of reproducing your work in small quantities. Photocopying can be done onto a wide variety of coloured papers and calligraphy can also be copied with a limited range of coloured toners. Always prepare all your work for photocopying in black and white. There have been rapid developments in colour photocopying particularly, so it is worth talking to your local copy shop to see what they can offer.

Photocopying paste-ups saves time. Make sure the originals are clean – cover up any marks with white correction fluid. If you need to cut down the work once it is copied, mark the edges with trim marks outside the corners of the work.

If you want to copy in two colours, say black and red, you have three choices. The first and cheapest course is to write and copy the black writing, and then to use a red pen or ink for the colour. The second option is to use a sophisticated colour photocopier. The third and most expensive route is to have the piece printed in two colours. The work must be prepared on two pieces of paper, with the words aligned and matching trim marks on both pieces.

You can use photocopiers to reduce or enlarge your work. Reduction is particularly useful if you need to produce something very small that is more easily done at a larger scale. Reducing work often improves its appearance. Scale up your work as shown from its finished size (A) by taking a diagonal line through it.

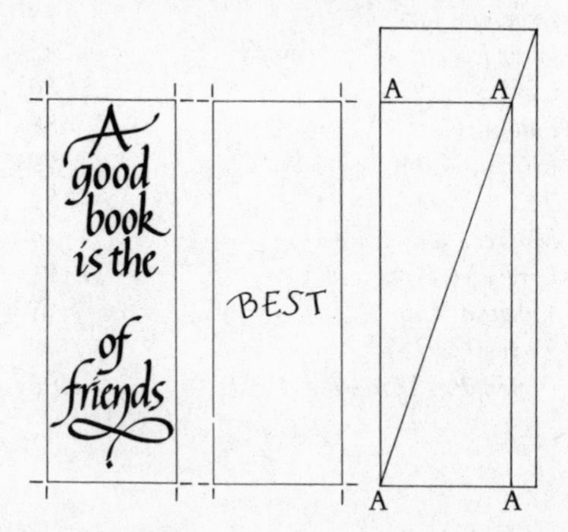

THE PROJECTS

DECORATION & ORNAMENTS

With a few simple strokes you can produce some effective patterns with the edged pen to give a decorative element which can be used with your designs for greetings cards and labels. Start with basic patterns made from straight, diagonal and curved shapes and then develop and combine them into individual designs.

Create a chequered pattern with alternating squares formed with the whole edge of the pen; these squares are the same as those you would make to measure up for the x-height of a letter.

Vary the pattern by making two strokes in the centre of the design. A straight line interrupted by some small diamond-shaped strokes gives a simple border.

The basic squares, circles and triangles that you wrote to discover how the pen works can be used as an effective pattern. The squares and circles are made with the pen at a flat angle, using the same pen for both large and small shapes. The triangles are written in a more random way, using slightly varying pen angles, and giving the line a bit of a curve.

A sequence of diagonals, or of curves, written in an anti-clockwise (or clockwise) direction, can be embellished with small diagonal strokes.

Follow the strokes to make a Greek key pattern with the pen at a flat angle.

To make a row of interlocking hearts, write a sequence of clockwise curves, diminishing at the end of the row if you like, to form one half. Now turn the paper through 90° so that you are looking at a vertical column and complete the other half of the hearts at the same angle.

Two crossed curves, and a dot for the eye, can be repeated to make a school of fish.

Leaves can be made in a similar way, but turn the paper so that the stalks (which are made first with a thinner pen) are vertical.

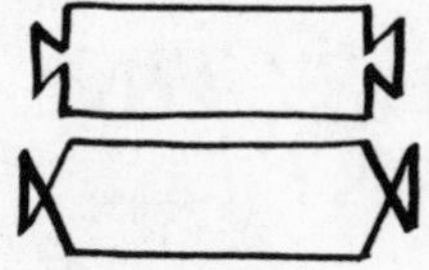

Borders for labels, or for headings for text, should be sketched in pencil first and then made with the pen held at a constant angle. Draw the longest lines first, freehand or with a ruler.

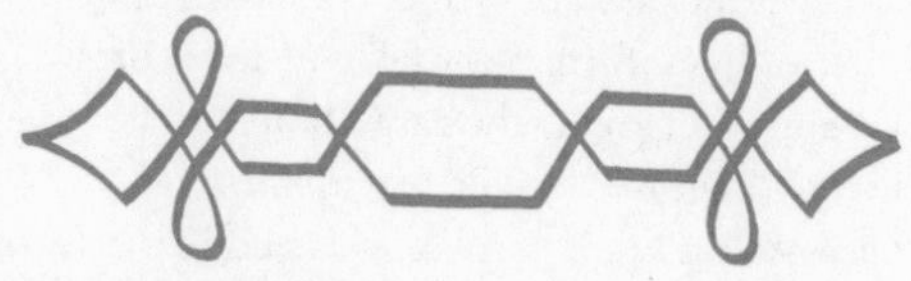

Work on this decorative ornament so that it is vertically positioned. Draw it first, then follow the strokes through with the pen, making the curved loops on either side in one movement. Try altering the proportions of the design.

These festive scrolls can be used at any size. Draw one and then trace it in reverse. Make sure that the curves flow as if they were ribbons.

LETTER PATTERNS

Letter forms, from the simplest to the most ornate, can be used and enjoyed not only for any message that you may want to write down, but also as pure decorative pattern.

Here, the capitals 'V' and 'A' are written in their simplest form, very tall with a fine or medium pen giving the barest bones of the letters. Repeated in a block with no space between the lines, the diagonals build up to form a pleasing pattern, the slight changes in the spacing giving some movement to the design. You could try filling the spaces with colour or with further lines that echo the shapes of the letters.

A pattern such as this could be used for your initials as a border around a letter, or, on a larger scale, you could cover a really large area and use the paper to wrap a gift for a friend.

Roundhand see pages 16-29

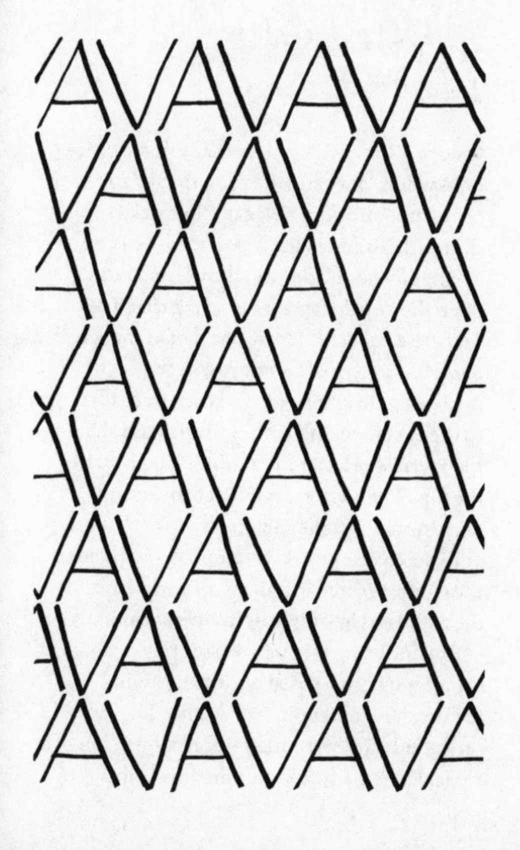

ENVELOPES & LETTERS

Calligraphic envelopes, perhaps with some decoration, or even a drawing that relates to the stamp not only looks elegant, but will cheer up the postman and make his or her job easier!

The envelope opposite above has a rather over-the-top device for declaring that it requires first class delivery. Draw one half of the scroll in pencil on a piece of layout paper, trace it in reverse on the other side and then trace through to the envelope. Ink in the outlines and shading, then write the lettering, diminishing towards the top. The address, is written in a simple, fairly heavy weight italic.

In the envelope below, emphasis is given to the name, written in italic with a wide nib, and the address is in simple lightweight capitals.

On the next pages you can see how a touch of calligraphy can be used with your own handwriting to emphasize words. The initial 'J' on the envelope is a rather informal version of a versal letter written with a medium nib.

Italic see pages 32-37

Bob Hankin
10 Park Drive
Oxford

Tina Callow
132 WEST AVENUE
CAMBRIDGE

Sunday
Dear Sandy
this is truly my
F·A·V·O·U·R·I·T·E
P·L·A·C·E
Wish you were here!
with lots of love
Su

Sandy Garfield
4 The Mansions
Hampstead Road
London N.W.5.

Joanna Isles
the Old Tea Shop
Burford
OXFORDSHIRE

November 7th

Dear Jo

Welcome back from your travels! I can't wait to hear all your news and to see your snaps

T·U·E·S·D·A·Y

D·E·A·R

Ken

THANK YOU

for the wonderful and most generous present. I was really

DOOR PLATES

You can identify your room with a calligraphic sign written on a piece of sturdy card. The sign can be glued to the door, or fixed with drawing pins.

Here, the design at the top is written in italics, with a border of pen-made fishes which meet at the centre. To do this, mark the centre of the card at the top and bottom in pencil and draw the fish with a pen on the right side of the card only. When you have completed this side, start again at the top from the nose of the first fish on the other side.

The middle sign is written in roundhand leaving enough space on either side of the name for brightly coloured drawing pins which are used to fix the sign to the door. Leaves and flowers, drawn with a fine pen add a decorative touch.

Signs for office doors should be less ornate. Names and messages, such as 'PRIVATE', written in a simple calligraphic hand are more attractive than typewritten labels.

Italic see pages 32-37   Roundhand see pages 16-29

PRIVATE

BADGES

These ideas are for birthdays (for children of all ages) and for other fun occasions. Of course, badges are often used for conferences and other meetings where people need to be identified. These would call for a rather restrained treatment.

You can buy badges made from card, with safety pins attached, that can be written on. There are also badge-making services, which will make up a proper metal badge for you from your own artwork. It is very simple, however, to make your own badge. Cut two discs of the same size out of medium-weight card, thread a large safety pin through one. Write your message on the second piece and then glue it to the first piece, making sure that the safety pin is in the right place to allow the message to be read! If you want the badge to last for some time, seal it with a layer of sticky-backed adhesive film.

Italic see pages 32-37 Roundhand see pages 16-29

I am 5
John
40 today
21 AGAIN
HELLO

BOOKMARK

A small project where just a few words can be arranged decoratively to make a thoughtful and useful present for a friend.

The thin, vertical shape of bookmarks determines the layout of the words in a column, and they are given a lively look through the use of flourishes; the words are written only on a base line (with a large pen), allowing the letters to take their own size. The italic is written with an x-height of 4 nib-widths, giving a heavy weight. The word 'BEST' is emphasized by writing capitals with a thin pen and tiny serifs that bounce along the line at different angles. The flourish at the bottom is made with one movement, and a dot added.

This project could be written in different colours on a stiff coloured paper, or it could be photocopied if you want to make several copies. To make it last longer, cover it with a thin sealing film.

Italic see pages 32-37

A good book is the BEST of friends

BOOKPLATE

Rather than simply writing your name in the front of your books, design a label that will identify them when you lend them to friends, to ensure their safe return to your library (the books not the friends . . .).

This label uses the latin, *ex libris* (from the books of) as the main element of the design, adapting the letter forms so that they form a pleasing pattern. The 'E' is large and rounded, the 'X' curves down to line up with the two 'I's below, and there is a common shape in the top of the 'R' and 'B'. The name is written in simple lightweight capitals, spaced so that both names fill the same space.

Labels can be written individually and pasted into books with a water-based glue or printed onto gummed paper.

Roundhand see pages 16-29

EX·LIBRIS
PAUL
EVERARD

TABLE LABELS

Brighten up a party table with some exuberant labels in the shape of scrolls and banners to help your guests make their choice from your feast.

To make the cheese labels, first write out the words and then design or copy one of the scrolls opposite leaving enough space for the lettering, using a fine or medium pen and cartridge paper. In order to fold the end of the label around a cocktail stick, change the outline as shown below and then cut accurately just beyond the pen line all around the outside of the scroll. Now write the name of the cheese on the label, then fold it down the vertical dotted line. Glue the scroll inside the fold and insert a cocktail stick.

The sandwich labels are simply cut from pieces of cartridge paper, the words written on them, and then a cocktail stick threaded through.

Fold here

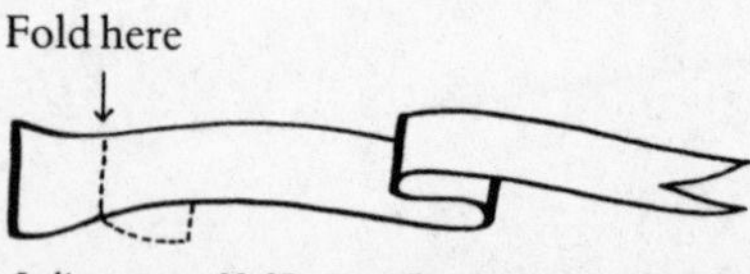

Italic see pages 32-37 Roundhand see pages 16-29

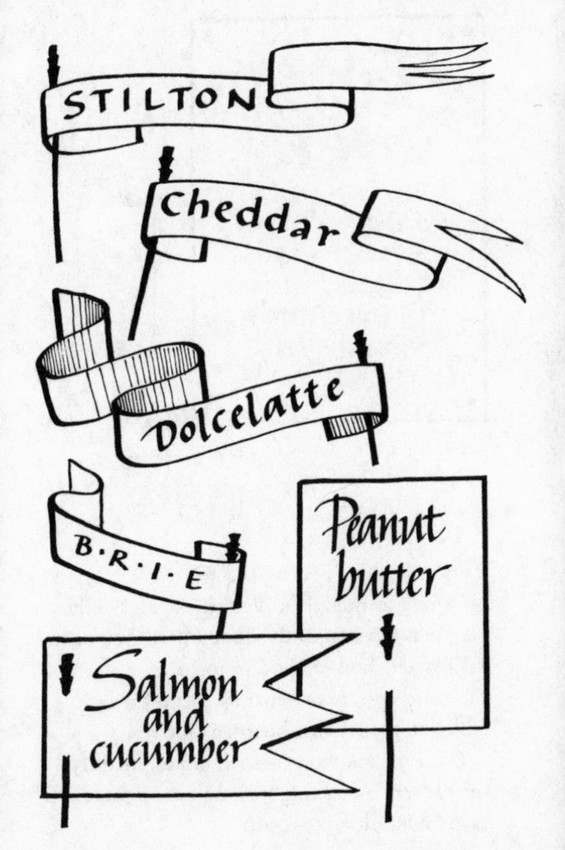
STILTON
Cheddar
Dolcelatte
B·R·I·E
Peanut
butter
Salmon
and
cucumber

PLACE NAMES

If you are giving a formal dinner it is helpful to provide a seating plan. Write the names of the people as seated near the door where they can be easily seen. This can be done on one very large sheet of paper, or on separate sheets for each table and pinned on a board, as above.

Once the guests are at their tables, identify their places by writing their names on pieces of card folded along the centre.

Place-name cards can also be made so that the names sit along the top of the card in relief.

The method is quite simple. First write out the names with a wide pen. With a pencil, mark on a piece of card a baseline, the x-height line and a line about ¼in (½cm) beyond that. Now rule a line on the other side of the baseline the same distance away as the last line you drew on the opposite side. Fold along the baseline, then lay the paper flat *(see below left)*.

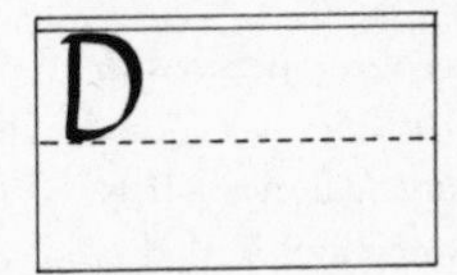

Write the name and carefully cut around the letters with a very sharp knife. Remove the counters (the bits of cards between the letters) *(see above)*, then fold back the waste card.

LABELS FOR JARS

Labelling your own home produce gives a special personal touch to a gift for a friend. You can use self-adhesive or sticky-backed labels, adapting them to your own design by cutting them into different shapes, or by adding borders and motifs. Alternatively, glue the paper to the jars. If you want, you can varnish the labels or spray them with fixative to prevent them smudging.

Express the mood or flavour or derivation of the produce that you are labelling.

The shape of the chutney and honey labels opposite have obvious connections with the contents; the honey jar is further embellished with a swarm of light-hearted pen-drawn bees.

On the next two pages are some ideas for herb labels, written in italic, with swooping capitals and descenders.

The spice labels on the second page overleaf are written with stylized angular capitals edged with dots to suggest the exotic origins of the spices. The borders are based on the shapes of the spices themselves.

Roundhand see pages 16-29

Apple
chutney

HONEY

Parsley
Sage
Rosemary
Thyme

Italic see pages 32-37

CORIANDER

CARAWAY

WINE LABELS

Reflect the character of the drink you are labelling in the lettering and decoration. For instance, elderflower champagne is light and bubbly, and is written here with a thin pen for italic with a tall x-height and a rather wayward flourish; the small serifed capitals are written with a very fine pen, with tiny dots between each letter to add to the lightness.

Elderberry wine is heavy, red and fruity, and this is reflected in the lettering with its rounded 'E's; the letters of the word 'wine' are also alternated with dots, but the scale is much larger and heavier than for the champagne.

Sloe gin is written with a chunky roundhand and rounded capitals; a series of curves around the label is elaborated at the top and bottom with shapes that call sloe berries to mind.

Peach leaf wine, blackberry wine, cider and other popular home brews offer plenty of inspiration for very different styles of calligraphy. You could try working a pretty illustration of the original fruit into your calligraphy design.

Italic see pages 32-37   Roundhand see pages 16-29

ELDERBERRY
·W·I·N·E·

If you feel that your vintage has pretensions to grandeur, say so in your label! The name of this 'chateau-bottled wine' is written with a large pen in a rather rounded gothic, with decorated initials. The light flourishes above and below provide a contrast in weight to the name, and link with the weight of the writing below.

Draw the flourishes in pencil first and then draw them in one sweeping movement with the pen. Flourishes are easier to write with fibre pens than with dip pens; if you are using the latter, stop and re-start at the thin parts of the strokes if the curves are not flowing well.

If you are having your wine label printed you could have the artwork 'reversed out' as here. The label was written in black ink on white paper, but the printing process literally reverses the colours.

Gothic see pages 38-40

Chateau
Barker
MIS EN BOUTEILLES
AU CHATEAU
12·5% vol.
75 cl.

CARDS

Greetings cards give scope for a myriad of design ideas, and, being on a small scale and of a personal nature, make very popular projects; they also give great pleasure to the people who receive them.

You may just want to write the greeting inside a printed card. Until you are confident about spacing and planning, work out the wording on a separate piece of paper before ruling up the card lightly in pencil and then writing your greeting.

The examples opposite show two fairly simple Christmas card designs. The card above is written in italic, with a row of pen-drawn Christmas trees, which, from a distance, look like another line of writing. Gothic is a popular choice of lettering for this festive greeting. Keep the line-spacing tight to create a dense look to the lettering and decorate the initial.

These cards are simple enough to write out in fairly large quantities, but to save time, you could photocopy them, or have them printed.

Best wishes
for
Christmas

and the
New Year

Christmas
greetings

FOLDING CARDS

Whether you are going to send the original card, or have it printed, it is useful to know how to take advantage of various methods of paper folding and plan your design accordingly.

Below, you can see how to arrange the lettering so that, when folded, writing appears on the front and on the inside of the card. Fold from A to A and B to B, so that the open edge is the one that stands on the table. Messages can be added to the inside front and back of the card. Use a medium weight paper for this design so that it folds easily.

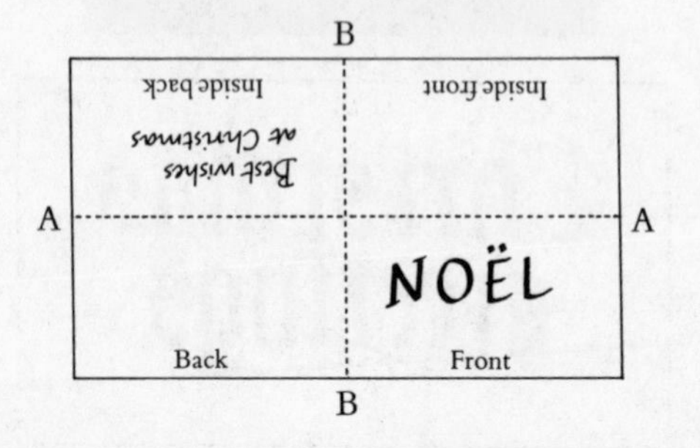

Italic see pages 32-37 Gothic see pages 38-40

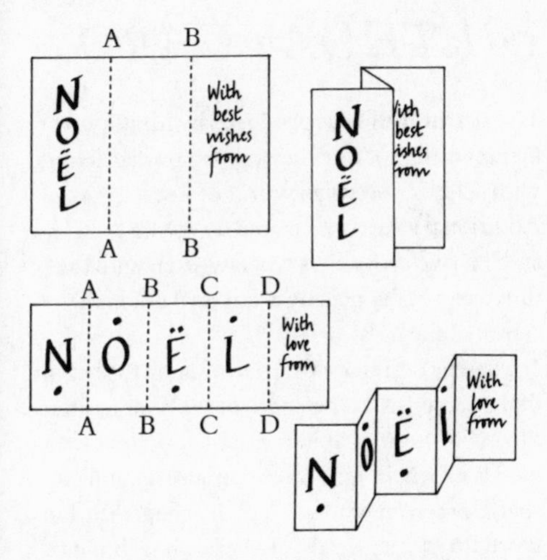

By making two vertical folds in opposite directions you will have scope for up to three writing areas. This idea can be carried through by using multiple folds, which can be particularly effective if the 'page' size is quite small. Each page can carry a single letter, with the greeting on the last page. The message can, of course, continue onto the other side of the paper. This idea can be used to make a zig-zag book, such as the alphabet book project.

BIRTHDAY CARD

This textural effect is produced by using two pens of different thicknesses for alternate letters with no space between words or lines. Additional interest is created by giving each 'A' and 'H' two cross-bars when written with the thin pen, and by placing a diagonal dot in the centre of the 'O's.

Plan the design by first deciding on the height of the capitals and the width of the design. Draw a base line for the capitals and then write out the words in pencil, ignoring word breaks and spaces between words. Here, by chance the last word fitted very neatly on the last line, but if this had not happened, the wording at the end could have been changed to fit. Now write the first and all alternate letters with a wide pen. Then write the remaining letters with a thin pen. Finally, put dots in the 'O's.

Roundhand see pages 16-29

HAPPYBIRT
HDAYTOYO
UHAPPYBIR
THDAYTOY
OHAPPYBIR
THDAYDEAR
EMMAHAPP
YBIRTHDAY
TOYOUWITH
LOVEFROM
SAMANTHA

THANK YOU CARD

Heavily textured watercolour paper was used for this card which was written with a wide pen. This has the effect of breaking up the line which adds to the decorative quality. Filling in the counters with additional strokes and repeating the word upside down further accentuates the card's decorative qualities.

Plan the design in pencil. Starting with large simple capitals, write the word 'THANKS', with the letters arranged vertically down the centre of the page. Turn the paper upside down and repeat the word on either side in the opposite direction.

With a wide red pen, write the central word, filling the counter spaces of the letters with additional strokes radiating out from the letter as you go. Now complete the words on either side with a black pen.

Roundhand see pages 16-29

THANKS

MOTHER'S DAY CARD

Send your mother a calligraphic bunch of flowers (and real flowers) to show you care.

The bow, the flowers and the word 'MOTHER'S' were done with a large fibre tip pen which has had a notch cut out of the middle of the nib with a sharp knife. This produces a double line and a very effective decorative effect – try out your modified pen before planning the design to see how it works. The letters will need fairly large serifs to complete the strokes.

Do the writing first, and plan the design around it. The words 'HAPPY' and 'DAY' are written with a medium pen to give emphasis to the word 'MOTHER'S'.

The bird holding on to the tail of the letter 'Y' was drawn with a fine pen. Move the paper so that the thick and the thin strokes flow smoothly around the shapes.

The bow and the flowers fill the space at the bottom of the card, and the ribbons on either side 'frame' it and link the bird at the top.

Roundhand see pages 16-29

HAPPY
MOTHER'S
DAY

FORGET ME NOT CARD

A sentimental message that has the appearance of a cross-stitch sampler is built up from a series of 'x's, which the more romantically inclined may regard as kisses! This design could also be used as the basis for a piece of embroidery.

Plan the design in pencil in large capitals with plenty of space all around them, forming a good pattern on the page.

Use a fine or medium pen to make the crosses, always trying to make them intersect on the pencil line, to preserve the shape of the letters. Start with a cross at the ends of stems to define each letter shape. This is particularly important where diagonals meet other lines, such as in the 'N' and 'M'. Keep the number of crosses in stems of similar types (eg three for the top cross-bar of the 'E' and 'F', two for the middle cross-bar) fairly consistent but don't be too rigid about it.

This would look effective if different coloured pens were used for the crosses, alternating red and green, for instance.

Roundhand see pages 16-29

FOR-
GET
ME
NOT

VALENTINE CARD

An illustration found in a scrap book was the inspiration for this valentine card.

Photocopy the illustration to the size you require onto a paper that you know you can write on, or trace it, or make your own drawing.

Work out the design of the lettering within the heart shape on a piece of layout paper. The lettering is a simple italic. The flourishes that fill the heart and echo the design of the girl's bodice are similar to one another, but are adapted to fill the space available and to flow from the letters. Draw them in pencil first and then try them out in ink, changing the angle of the paper until the weight of the pen falls as you require.

When you are happy with the design, transfer it onto the drawing.

Italic see pages 32-37

To my
valentine

ZODIAC CARD

♈	♉	♊	♋
Aries	Taurus	Gemini	Cancer
♌	♍	♎	♏
Leo	Virgo	Libra	Scorpio
♐	♑	♒	♓
Sagittarius	Capricorn	Aquarius	Pisces

To draw the sign of Aries (opposite) on a large scale, you can use double pencils. Smooth out the curve where the lines cross (see below), and then use a fine pen to fill in the shape with dots. Rub out the pencil marks. Write the capitals, then use a red pen for the constellation and other dots. Finally, draw the borders.

Roundhand see pages 16-29

PERSONALIZED GREETINGS CARD

A personalized greetings card with this highly decorated initial is truly a labour of love. The curious letter form, constructed from five fishes, is borrowed from an old illuminated manuscript. Old books can provide a rich, inventive, and often amusing source of inspiration for illuminated letters and can be found reproduced in books, or in museums.

To make the 'E', first draw the large outline curve of the letter in pencil and then draw in the bodies, fins and tails with a fine pen. Then draw the 'cross-bar' fish outline. Put in the eyes and the gills, and then decorate the 'serif' tails.

Now for the scales. Turn the paper so that the nose of one of the fish is facing you and draw rows of continuous curves beyond the gills. The name is written in versal capitals.

Versals see pages 30-31

EDMUND

DECORATIVE INITIALS

This dragon has wound himself into a fanciful letter 'S'. He would make an ideal design for a card for someone whose name begins with 'S', or perhaps for a patriotic Englishman or woman on St George's Day.

He can be copied either by tracing the outline or by photocopying. You may prefer to draw him from scratch though, in which case you should start by drawing a central s-shaped curve, then build the body from this main structure. Pencil in the outline and then go over it with a fine pen. The shading is put in last, and is used in those areas that would be in shadow if the light source came from the right of the page. This gives the dragon a three-dimensional effect.

Other mythical and fantastic creatures can be similarly treated calligraphically – griffins, sphinxes, satyrs and so on – you can pick your creature carefully to convey a particular message to the recipient of the calligraphy.

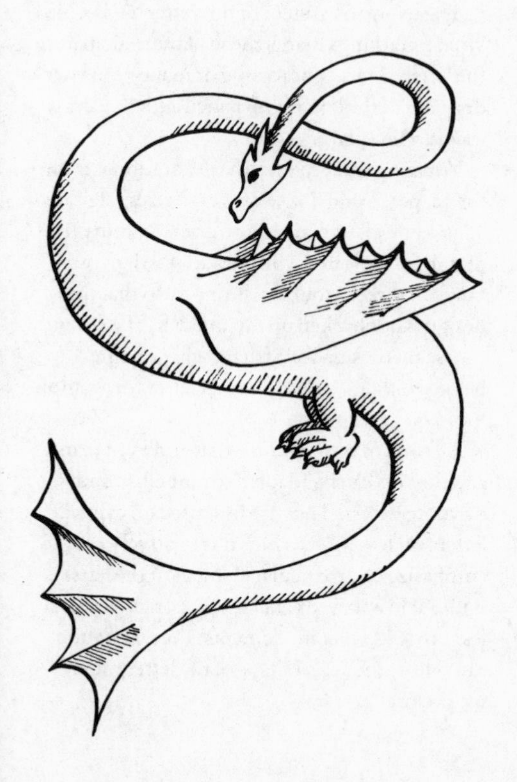

The overgrown stem of this letter 'G' is a bird whose markings match those of the main part of the letter. Trace, photocopy or make your own drawing of the letter with pencil and then draw it with a fine pen.

You may want to vary the decoration within the shapes, using dots, squares, circles, zig zags. This could also be made into a very colourful design, but it is probably best to restrict your range to three colours at the most, so that the design is not broken up too much by the colour.

Use this design for a friend whose name begins with 'g', or as the initial letter for a simple message, 'greetings'.

All sorts of birds and animals and even plants and flowers can be adapted to embellish and decorate letters. They are best used on capital letters such as 'G' in which it is relatively easy to emphasize one particular element of the letter without losing its overall form. For letters with less obvious separate elements, the decoration can follow the actual shape of the letter much more closely.

MONTHLY AND PERPETUAL CALENDARS

When designing a calendar you will first have to plan how the months will be arranged; all on one large poster, grouped in twos or threes, or one month per page. There should be some constant design element throughout, such as how the weeks are arranged, or the inclusion of a quotation that relates to each month. The pages can be held together by string threaded through a punched hole at the top or spiral binding.

The April calendar opposite is designed on a landscape format that will accommodate all the names of the months written on a large scale. The days of the week were planned first, written with a medium pen, and this determined the space available for the heavily weighted heading and the lightweight cursive quote.

On the next page is a design for the first two pages of a perpetual calendar for June. The amount of space for each day can be varied as required.

Italic see pages 32-37

April

April, April. Laugh thy girlish laughter.

Monday		2	9	16	23	30
Tuesday		3	10	17	24	
Wednesday		4	11	18	25	
Thursday		5	12	19	26	
Friday		6	13	20	27	
Saturday		7	14	21	28	
Sunday	1	8	15	22	29	

BIRTHDAYS & ANNIVERSARIES IN June

1

2

3

4

5

6

Italic see pages 32-37

◆
◆
7
◆
◆
8
◆
◆
9
◆
◆
10
◆
◆
11
◆
◆
12
◆
◆
13
◆
◆
14

ADVENT CALENDAR

To make this advent calendar, start by drawing the outline of the design in pencil, making sure that you allow for 25 windows. Copy it onto two pieces of card of the same size, in exactly the same position so that they can be superimposed on top of one another. The top one is shown; the lower one will have illustrations on it.

On one piece of card, ink in the outlines, write the numbers and then shade in the needles on the tree as shown opposite. Now cut around the shapes as shown below, to allow for openings in the windows.

Trace the shapes of the windows onto another piece of paper and fill them with little illustrations and cut them out.

Glue all of the second piece of card and stick the illustrations in position. Place the top piece of card in position and press down.

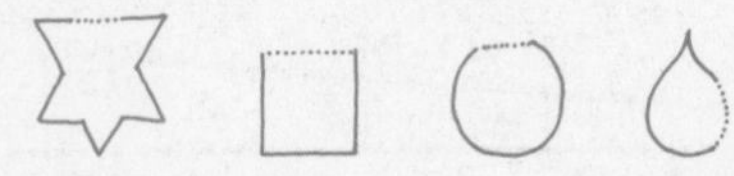

1
2
3
4
5
6
7
8
9
10
11
12
13
14
15
16
17
18
19
20
21
22
23
24
25

WEDDING AND CHILDREN'S PARTY INVITATIONS

The style, theme or mood of your party can be reflected in a calligraphic invitation. When you are planning the design, think about the availability of envelopes of the correct size.

The formal wedding invitation opposite is in a traditional style, appropriate for an important occasion. To help you to achieve symmetry in the design, write out the text and cut and paste up the lines in position. Emphasize the names by writing them with a larger pen and by leaving more space around them. The address is written with a very thin pen.

On the next page is a children's party invitation which uses balloons to contain the design. Draw the balloons freehand, or use compasses or draw around a small round object. To write around a curved line, first draw a curved pencil baseline and turn the paper round as you write. The left hand page can be torn off and used for the reply.

Italic see pages 32-37

Mr and Mrs Alan Jones
invite you to celebrate
the marriage of

Thomas Smith
to
Amanda

at St Margaret's Church
Bampton, Somerset
on April 1st at 12 noon
and afterwards at The Red House

R.S.V.P. THE RED HOUSE, BAMPTON

Roundhand see pages 16-29

Ben and Helen
invite you
to a
·P·A·R·T·Y·
on August 20th
at 3 o/clock
at
512 Dover Road
Preston
· RSVP ·

FIREWORKS PARTY INVITATION

The sparks that fly off a Catherine wheel formed the basis of this idea for a fireworks party invitation.

Mark a central point on the paper and use a roll of tape or a flexible rule as a template to draw the radiating lines in pencil from this point. Use a fine pen and do the black writing first, then the red writing, along the pencil lines, using long curved ascenders to add to the sparks. Finally, put in the dots in the centre of the design.

If you want to have this printed, you should separate the colours. Write the words you want in black on one piece of paper and the words you want printed in red in black on another piece of paper. (NB Both sets of words must be written in black.) Make sure that you plot accurately how the design should be printed, using trim marks.

Italic see pages 32-37

Andrew and Chloe
invite you to
a fireworks party
on November 5th
from 7·30 p.m.
at River House, Freshfield
please bring a bottle
and a firework
remember, remember
the fifth
of November
gunpowder, treason
and plot

CHANGE OF ADDRESS CARD

Notification of a change of address does not have to be a dull affair. Here the announcement is made loud and clear by the words and with the simple, cartoon-like drawing of the new house.

The information is divided into two parts, balanced diagonally across the design, linked by the drawing of the house. Plenty of space is left at top right and bottom left, contrasting with the tight margins around the writing. The informal versal letters at the top are used on a smaller scale in the name of the person, written with the same fine pen. Simple capitals are used for the address, and a line space is left between the address and the telephone number.

A change of address may be printed or photocopied onto paper or card. Remember when designing it to make sure that you can get envelopes of the right size for your design.

Versals see pages 30-31   Roundhand see pages 16-29

CHANGE OF ADDRESS

MARK EVANS

39 HARBOUR DRIVE
PLYMOUTH
DEVON

TEL: 0732 4231

BIRTH ANNOUNCEMENT

The birth of a new baby is an important occasion that can be announced in a friendly way with calligraphy.

This asymmetrical arrangement divides the information into two main text areas, balanced diagonally from top left to bottom right of the card. The rather bemused pen-drawn stork links the two. The lines of text are rather randomly arranged and writing lines have been ignored to some extent to increase the sense of informality.

If you want to make many copies, and you want to use a second colour, this can be done inexpensively by photocopying everything that will appear in black, leaving a space for the name, and then writing the name in colour on the copies.

To print it in two colours, present the printer with two separate pieces of artwork, one for the black writing, one for the other colour (but written in black). Indicate how to align them and the second colour you want.

Italic see pages 32-37

Fred and Linda Parker
are happy to announce
the birth of
a baby girl

Sabina
was born on
22nd November
weighing 7lb 11oz

ALPHABET BOOK

An illustrated alphabet concertina book makes a decorative and instructive gift for a young child; it can also be adapted to make a wall frieze.

Use simple lettering, such as these roundhand capitals and small letters, and choose the animals to illustrate the letters. Plan the design for the title page and a sample page for the letters.

When you have decided on the measurement of the page you can estimate the amount of paper required (use a fairly stout paper so that it will stand up to handling). These instructions are for an alphabet that is written on both sides of 14 pages. On one side you will have the title page and letters up to 'M'; on the other side will be 'N' to 'Z' and a final blank page, where you can write a personal message. So if, for instance, the width of the page is 4½ inches (11.5cm); you will need a total length of 63 inches (161cm). Unless you use a roll of paper you will need to add extra allowances of ¼ inch (½cm) on both sides of all joins. Mark and cut out the paper and pencil in the design. When you have penned the writing and the drawing, glue the joins neatly.

Roundhand see pages 16-29

AN
ANIMAL

A B
C

ALPHABET

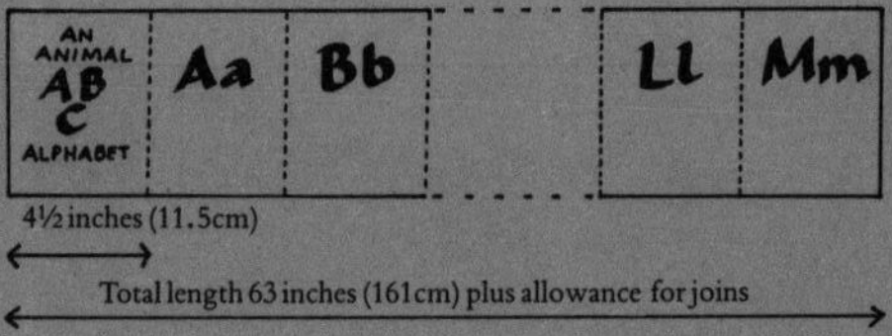

AN ANIMAL AB C ALPHABET	Aa	Bb		Ll	Mm

4½ inches (11.5cm)

Total length 63 inches (161cm) plus allowance for joins

Aa

ant

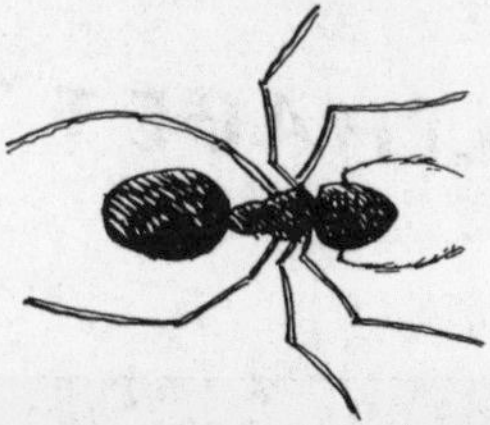

Roundhand see pages 16-29

Bb

bat

Cc

cat

Dd

duck

FAVOURITE RECIPE

The next time a friend asks you to pass on a particularly delicious recipe, why not write it down in an attractive way, rather than scribbling it on a scrap of paper. It may then find its way from the pages of a recipe book to the kitchen pin board.

This recipe for peperonata is set out quite simply. The title is written with a large pen and this determined the width of the whole piece. A fine pen was used for all the roundhand writing, the drawing and the border. The ingredients at the top are slightly indented from the left-hand margin, and the drawing fills the space to the right. The line spacing is quite tight, so care must be taken to avoid ascenders and descenders colliding. The words have a ragged right-hand margin. If you want it to align on this side you would have to hyphenate the words. In the final line the word 'and' is abbreviated to a '+' sign to avoid making an extra line of text. Borders of tiny circles add a decorative finishing touch.

Roundhand see pages 16-29

PEPERONATA

8 red peppers
10 tomatoes
2 onions
2 cloves garlic
2 bay leaves
olive oil
salt and pepper

Chop the onions and garlic finely and fry gently in the oil with the bay leaves for about 15 minutes.

De-seed the peppers, remove the skin by burning it off over a flame, then slice coarsely. Peel and chop the tomatoes. Add the peppers and the tomatoes to the pan and cook for another 15 minutes. Season + serve.

COCKTAIL RECIPE

A cocktail recipe is a more unusual subject for calligraphy but it offers scope for a rather interesting and decorative design.

The cocktail glass is drawn with a large pen in just a few quick strokes – the right-hand edge of the glass is simply implied. The salt placed around the rim in this and so many other cocktails, whether tequila-based or not, is depicted by some dots with a thin pen. The name of the cocktail is written in capitals that bounce in a drunken (or merry) manner across the page. Written in black, the letters would dominate the whole design too much, so a red pen was used instead to reduce some of the weight of the letters while giving colour contrast at the same time. The ingredients are written in simple capitals with a fine pen with just enough line space between them to create a dense texture while retaining legibility.

Roundhand see pages 16-29

2 OZ TEQUILA
½ OZ TRIPLE SEC
JUICE OF ½ LIME

MARGARITA

SHAKE THOROUGHLY WITH
CRACKED ICE, STRAIN INTO A
COCKTAIL GLASS RIMMED WITH SALT.

MENU

Commemorate a special celebratory dinner with a calligraphic menu which can be signed by all the guests at the table and kept as a souvenir of the evening.

The style of this menu suggests the mood of the evening – it will be fun and informal. For a more formal occasion, the design and lettering should be more restrained.

Here, the word 'menu' is written at a steep angle, the letters jumping up and down on the writing line. The double stem effect is achieved by writing the word with a medium nib first to produce the thick stems which can then be echoed with lines drawn using a fine nib; the serifs are finally added to the 'u' and 'n'. The simple, widely spaced capitals were written with a thin pen. Finally, all the dots were made, giving a sparkle and movement to the page. You may prefer to add the dots to the design once it has been photocopied if you use a paper of a fairly dark tone. A gold or silver pen or paint would look very effective.

Italic see pages 32-37

Parsnip + apple soup

Rainbow trout

Passion fruit brulée

10 MAY

NOTICES

Notices, posters and signs must be eye-catching, striking and clear. You should know exactly where the notice is going to be placed so that you can plan your design appropriately. If, for instance, the sign is going to be pinned to a cluttered noticeboard, the best thing you can do is make your sign as simple as possible with plenty of space around the margins so that it is well framed.

Capitals have an authority which makes them a good choice for the lettering. Think about using colour. Red is particularly strong. If the notice is being hung indoors, you do not have to worry about the effects of the weather. Protect an outdoor notice with transparent film or have it laminated.

The two signs opposite declare their messages simply. Hang the straightforward 'DO NOT DISTURB' notice on a door and it won't be misunderstood. The 'WAY OUT' sign above has a rather more humorous touch with the pen-drawn hand and more lively capitals.

Roundhand see pages 16-29

DO NOT DISTURB

JUMBLE SALE SIGN

Advertisements for jumble sales, fetes, car boot sales and the like need to say exactly what is happening and when and where.

You may also want to add some details about what will be offered, but the most important consideration is that such advertisements should be striking. Make sure that the information is uncluttered – leave unimportant details out and plenty of space round the information that you do put in so that it is very legible from a distance.

The zig-zag borders provide a frame that will catch the eye and were done using the thick and the thin edges of the nib.

The incorporation into the calligraphy of a simple illustration showing what is for sale, if that is what the sign is advertising, can really be very eye-catching. If the sign is to be hung outdoors, laminate it or seal it with adhesive film to protect it from the weather.

Roundhand see pages 16-29

SATURDAY
10 DECEMBER
FROM 12–4 PM

AT BEAUFORT SCHOOL

BEWARE OF THE DOG SIGN

This sign has a rather ambiguous message. At a first glance the layout and lettering appear to be designed to frighten would-be trespassers, but on closer examination the portrait of the canine terror and the lively nature of the lettering of the word 'DOG' betray something of its friendliness. Not all such notices need be quite so friendly if you are aiming for a very different effect though. Leaving the illustration out immediately makes the message more direct.

The letters are all pen written versals. Notice that the 'H' and 'E' in the word 'THE' are joined. This was something that was commonly practised in medieval manuscripts when words had to be made to fit into a line.

To draw the 'O' with the dog hanging over it, draw everything in pencil first, then draw the dog with the pen before inking in the letter.

Versals see pages 30-31

BEWARE OF THE DOG

CERTIFICATE

Certificates and diplomas are used to record achievements of all kinds. They are relatively formal documents and their design often benefits from simple treatment and an uncomplicated layout. Here, a golfer's hole in one is recorded for posterity.

The design is centred, with the majority of the writing done with a fine pen. Emphasis is given to the name with a wide pen, extra space, and a small flourish on the 'E' and the 'n'. 'Hole in one' is written with a medium pen in capitals at the same height as the x-height of the italics. Allow extra space at the bottom margin so that the design sits well within the frame.

There are papers that imitate parchment that would be suitable for this type of project.

Italic see pages 32-37

This is to
certify that

Eva Allen

had a
HOLE IN ONE
at the third hole
on 13th July
at
Wimbledon Golf Club

LETTERHEAD

To give an impression of professionalism, have your own personalized letterhead printed (or photocopied if you require small quantities).

When considering the design, take into account the image that you want to convey about yourself, and then think about the content – will you give your name as well as your address and phone number? If you are using the paper for business, remember to allow space for the address of the person you are writing to. There are standard paper and envelope sizes, so design to a relevant format and consider how the paper will fold in order to fit into the envelope.

Here, the name is the dominant part of the design, written with a large pen, as are the lines at the top and bottom of the page. The top line is broken by the 'S' and the descender of the 'p', which links the name with the address below, written with a fine pen in simple capitals. The writing is all ranged to the right of the page leaving space for the name and address of the addressee to be written on the left.

Italic see pages 32-37   Roundhand see pages 16-29

Stephen Hill

5 HAMPTON ST · NORWICH · NORFOLK
TEL: 0603 213465

ADDRESS CARD

Although cards can be designed to any format or dimensions, it is generally most convenient to produce one that is the same size as a credit card, so that it can be carried uncreased in a wallet.

Blank visiting cards can be bought from stationery shops and written individually, but you may want to consider preparing a design for reproduction as this can be a very useful item to have in large numbers.

When working towards such a small finished size, it is advisable to work on a larger scale and have your design reduced.

If you have also designed a letterhead, you could use the same design at a reduced size. However, reducing lettering by a very large proportion may distort the spacing and letter weight, so you may need to rework the design on a smaller scale.

Alternatively, you may like to adapt the design to incorporate a logo, such as the letters 'SH' opposite, loosely written superimposed capitals, written onto textured watercolour paper (and pasted onto the design).

Roundhand see pages 16-29

STEPHEN HILL
5 HAMPTON STREET
NORWICH·NORFOLK
TEL: 0603 213465

QUOTATIONS

Writing quotations, whether the sentiment is humorous or uplifting, can lead to interesting interpretation of the words. Carefully chosen, designed and framed, a thoughtful quotation can make a delightful gift for a friend.

Here, in this amusingly self-contradictory statement, each word shouts out from its own line. The longest word was written first and this determined the size of the letters. The simple, slightly narrow capital letters are written with a fine pen and most of the straight stems have tiny serifs. The letters are written quite freely and most of the horizontals sweep up towards the right to give a sense of movement. The line space varies, but in general is rather close.

It may take several attempts to achieve this seemingly casual arrangement, which has the appearance of symmetry without being centred. Mark the centre of the page with a vertical pencil line and then work down the page, balancing the distribution of the letters on either side of the centre with regard to the whole piece.

Roundhand see pages 16-29

IF
THERE'S
ONE
THING
I
CAN'T
STAND,
IT'S
INTOLERANCE

A SPANISH PROVERB

This wonderfully peaceful Spanish proverb is a calming reminder of how luxuriously slow the pace of life can be for some people.

The interpretation of texts is highly personal, but it tends to be generally accepted that a landscape, or horizontal format enhances a sense of calm. The lines are broken not only with regard to their visual arrangement, but also at a point where there is a natural break in the rhythm of the sentence. The text is written in italic; the large initial 'H' is written with a wider pen, and this is balanced on the other side with the long swooping tail of the 'g'. The capitals at the bottom are simple and light (written with a thin pen), so that they do not detract from or intrude on the quotation.

You may want to pick proverbs or sayings from each of the countries you have been on holiday in and vary the calligraphy to reflect the meaning of the different messages and the different qualities of the different countries.

Italic see pages 32-37

How beautiful it is to do nothing
and then to sit down again afterwards
and rest

·: SPANISH PROVERB :·

BIBLICAL QUOTATION

A reproduction of a medieval manuscript found in a book was the inspiration for the design of this biblical quotation.

The initial letter 'B' was photocopied from the book and enlarged to the right size for the piece. The lines of writing were then planned with fairly narrow line-spacing to emphasize the dense, textural effect of the gothic lettering. The fall of the words leaves an uneven edge on the right-hand side, which has been retained rather than evened up with hyphens. The attribution is written in small capitals, which gives a third contrast of weight to the piece.

The initial letter is a versal letter form. The outline was drawn with a red pen and then filled in, and the decoration was added last.

This traditional arrangement shows just one of the many ways to interpret this type of text – it would work just as well, but convey a different mood, if, for instance, it was written in light, well-spaced capitals.

Gothic see pages 38-40   Versals see pages 30-31

Better is
a handful of
quietness than
two full hands
of toil
ECCLESIASTES
4:6

SHAKESPEARE QUOTATION

Shakespeare must be one of the most quoted of all writers in the English language. This is one of the less often quoted lines from *As You Like It* which could well be hung on the wall as a reminder of the unpredictable course of love.

The layout of the piece is fairly simple, the italic text is written with a large pen at an x-height of 4 nib-widths with a space of one x-height between each baseline and the top of the x-height line below. The heavy writing is contrasted with the lighter weight letters at the bottom of the piece. The large flourished initial 'W' and the 'g' in the last line give a diagonal balance to the design.

The letter forms are quite freely written. The 'a' is an angular version of the arched roundhand 'a', the 'e' has an angular rather than a rounded bowl, the 'r' runs into the letter that follows it (except for 'a'). Letter height varies: the 'r' extends below the baseline and the second 'e' is noticeably smaller than the rest.

Series 536

THE LADYBIRD BOOK OF

GARDEN FLOWERS

By

BRIAN VESEY-FITZGERALD, F.L.S.

Colour Illustrations by

JOHN LEIGH-PEMBERTON

Publishers: Wills & Hepworth Ltd., Loughborough

First published 1960  *Printed in England*

Forsythia A hardy shrub which grows to twelve feet and blooms early in the year. It should be planted in the autumn in well-tilled soil. After flowering, the old wood must be cut out to make room for the new, which will flower the following year.

Chionadoxa A member of the Lily family. It flowers early in the year; often at the same time as the snowdrops. It is a very good plant for rockeries. Plant the bulbs in the autumn, three inches apart and one inch deep.

Christmas Rose This is not a rose, but a Hellebore. It is called the " Christmas Rose " because it is often in flower on Christmas Day. It should be planted in September in the shade. The best place is under the branches of a tree or among ferns.

Crocus A member of the Iris family. This is one of the easiest plants to grow, for it will do equally well in borders, in grass, or in bowls indoors. Put some bone meal in the holes when you plant the corms. Once planted, you can leave them for four years, but then they should be lifted and divided.

1 Forsythia
2 Chionadoxa
3 Christmas Rose
4 Crocus

Daffodil Most Daffodils can be grown in flower borders, in grass, or in bowls indoors. The bulbs should be planted in the autumn. Out-of-doors, large bulbs should be one foot apart and six inches deep; small bulbs six inches apart and one-and-a-half inches deep. They can then be left for five years before being lifted. After flowering, the leaves should be left to yellow off before they are cut.

Narcissus The only difference between a Narcissus and a Daffodil is, as you can see from the picture, that the Narcissus has not got a long trumpet. For planting and growing, the treatment is the same for both.

Tulip Tulips can be grown in flower borders or in bowls indoors, but they will not do well in grass. Put sand and bone meal in the holes when you plant the bulbs in the autumn, six inches deep and five inches apart. They can then be left for three years before lifting. After flowering, allow the leaves to yellow off before removing them.

Primula A member of the Primrose family. This hardy plant is very easy to grow from seed. Most of them prefer a rather damp soil and all of them do better if given some leaf-mould.

1 Daffodil
2 Narcissus
3 Tulip
4 Primula

Iris Reticulata A member of the Iris family, which grows from a bulb. The bulbs should be planted in August or September, in a sunny position, in rich, well-drained soil. Put them six inches apart and three inches deep. They should be lifted and replanted every three years.

Fritillary A member of the Lily family, commonly known as the Snake's-head Lily. The bulbs should be planted four inches deep in the autumn and some sand put in the holes. The Snake's-head Lily grows very well in grass and is also suitable for rockeries.

Polyantha A member of the Primrose family. It flowers in bunches and this distinguishes it from Primulas. The seed should be sown in March in John Innes Compost; the baby plants pricked out in a cold frame and then planted out in June. These should be lifted and replanted in their final positions in September, and can be increased by dividing the roots after flowering. They prefer a moist situation.

Grape Hyacinth A member of the Lily family. The plants are very easy to grow and are especially suitable for rockeries, though they do well in borders. Plant the bulbs in autumn, two inches deep and four inches apart.

1 Iris Reticulata
2 Fritillary
3 Polyantha
4 Grape Hyacinth

Magnolia The Lily-tree. One of the most beautiful of flowering shrubs. The one in the picture flowers in the spring and sheds its leaves for the winter. There are also a few varieties which are evergreen. All Magnolias should be planted in the spring. They need a good loamy soil, and grow better in sheltered positions.

Wallflower Though you may find it difficult to believe, this is a member of the Cabbage family. Deliciously scented, it will thrive on most soils and does not need manuring. Sow the seed in May or June, and when the plants appear, thin them out to one foot apart. Leave them until the autumn and then move them to the flower borders. They will flower the following summer.

Alyssum Another member of the Cabbage family. The dwarf plants are most suitable for rockeries, but they do not like a wet soil. Sow the seeds in March or April and they will flower the same year. Alyssums are perennials.

Forget-Me-Not A native British plant, which does especially well on chalk, but which will thrive on practically any soil in almost any situation. Sow the seeds in early summer. The plants will then be ready for transplanting in the autumn. After flowering, the plants can be increased by splitting them up.

1 Magnolia
2 Wallflower
3 Alyssum
4 Forget-Me-Not

Azalea One of the most brilliant of spring-flowering shrubs, and the leaf colour in the autumn is almost as brilliant. The shrubs like a peaty soil and do best in full sun, but with shelter from neighbouring trees and shrubs. They should be cut back after flowering, but you must get an expert to show you how to do this.

Tulip Here are two more varieties of the plant already described on page 6. These are grown in just the same way. There are a great many varieties of Tulips in all sorts of colours (except blue), so that with care they will bloom from March until late June.

Aubretia A member of the Cabbage family, which is sometimes known as Rock Cress. This is a very hardy, dwarf, evergreen plant, which does splendidly in rockeries or on the margins of flower beds. It produces a mass of bloom in early spring, and then flowers off and on through the summer and into the early autumn. Sow the seed under glass in March or out-of-doors in May.

Arabis Another member of the Cabbage family, which is also sometimes known as Rock Cress. It is cheap to buy and easy to grow, and is excellent for rockeries or for hanging over walls. It will flower in a mild winter, but is at its best in spring when it produces great masses of white bloom. It can easily be increased by division.

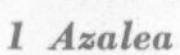

1 Azalea
2 Tulip
3 Aubretia
4 Arabis

Iris The name means the " Rainbow Flower ". It is one of the oldest cultivated plants, for its likeness appears on the tombs of the Egyptian Pharoahs. The one in the picture is a Tall Bearded Iris. The rhizomes (which correspond to bulbs in other plants) should be planted in October. Be careful not to bury them. They should be half-out of the soil, in the sunniest possible position. Irises need all the sun they can get. Do not be disappointed if they do not flower for two years. You can increase them by splitting the rhizomes and planting them separately in the autumn.

Peony Though difficult to believe, this is a member of the Buttercup family. It is a hardy perennial which requires good soil and also good staking. Plant in October and remember that Peonies like a fair amount of shade. You can increase by dividing the plants every four years.

Aquilegia Another member of the Buttercup family. Sow the seeds in a frame in spring and transplant them in the summer, when they will flower early in the following year. They are best grown in clumps. Once established they are perennial. They will flourish in almost any soil provided that they are well watered in dry weather.

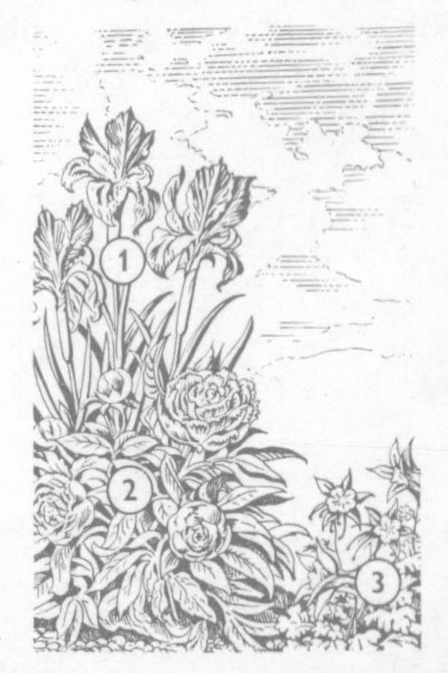

1 Iris
2 Peony
3 Aquilegia

Lupin Lupins are very hardy plants and will thrive in almost any soil. The seeds should be sown out-of-doors in early summer. They will then flower early in the following year. They are big plants and should be set three to four feet apart. They need staking to prevent them blowing over.

Sweet William A member of the Dianthus family. Sweet Williams are biennials: that is, they should be sown one year to flower the next, and then uprooted. Sow the seed in May. When the plants are transplanted they should be one foot apart. Sweet Williams do best on chalky soil. If the soil is not chalky, they need some lime.

Nigella Also known as Love-in-a-mist. Nigella is a hardy annual: it lives only one year. Sow the seed in spring out-of-doors in ordinary soil and, when the plants appear, thin them out to nine inches apart.

Pansy A member of the Violet family. Pansies are very easy to grow, for they will thrive in almost any soil so long as it is not too dry. The seeds should be sown out-of-doors in early summer. Once you have got Pansies going in your garden, they will seed themselves.

1 Lupin
2 Sweet William
3 Nigella
4 Pansy

Pyrethrum A member of the Chrysanthemum family. Pyrethrums are perennials (come up year after year) and make excellent plants for the flower border, for they will flower a second time if cut back after the first flowering. They can be increased by splitting up the clumps when they start growing.

Cornflower A native British plant which is a hardy annual. Sow the seed out-of-doors in ordinary soil in September or April. When the plants begin to grow, thin them out to one foot apart and stake them, or they may blow over.

Geum A member of the Rose family. Geums will thrive in almost any soil, flower in spring and early summer, and go on flowering for a long time. Sow the seed in boxes in summer to flower the following year. The plants should be set out one-and-a-half feet apart in May.

Stock Some Stocks are biennials and some are annuals. The seed of Brompton Stock, a biennial, should be sown out-of-doors in May to flower the following year. The great thing to remember about Stocks is that they should be planted thickly together.

Day Lily Each flower lasts only a day, but the plant will go on flowering for a very long time. Day Lilies are best planted in clumps one foot apart in a sunny position. They can be increased by splitting up the clumps in spring.

1 Pyrethrum *2 Cornflower*
3 Geum *4 Stock*
5 Day Lily

Hybrid Tea Rose The H.T. Roses, of which there are many varieties, are a modern development. Many are beautifully scented. They thrive on any well-drained soil, but need annual manuring. They are best planted in the autumn, and require hard pruning in the spring, at the end of March or early in April. Pruning is an art, and it is better to get an expert to show you how to do it the first time.

Floribunda Rose The name given to all those Roses which flower in clusters, having many flowers at the same time. They are very hardy and should be planted in the autumn. They do not require as hard pruning as the H.T. Roses, but again it is best to get an expert to show you how to do it.

Lavender A shrub famous for its scent. It will flourish on most soils, but is particularly fond of chalk. Plant two feet apart, either in the autumn or spring. You can get more plants by taking cuttings of the side shoots during the growing season.

Dianthus This is the Carnation family. The flowers in the picture are the very popular hybrids known as Allwoodii. The seed should be sown out-of-doors in summer. Once the plants are established, they can be increased by pulling young shoots out of the sockets of the old plants, and replanting them in sandy, moist soil in summer.

1 Hybrid Tea Rose
2 Floribunda Rose
3 Lavender
4 Dianthus

Delphinium A member of the Buttercup family. A tall perennial plant which flowers from June onwards. Delphiniums can be grown from seed, but it is better to get young plants. They require rich, well-drained soil and a sunny, but sheltered, position.

Gaillardia A member of the Daisy family. There are annual and perennial varieties. It is better to start with the annuals, which can be easily grown from seed. Sow the seed in the spring in light, fertile soil, and the plants will bloom profusely in the summer.

Gypsophila A hardy perennial, which will grow into a broad bush and is sometimes known as the "Chalk Plant". It is easily raised from seed sown in the spring, and will thrive in most soils, though it particularly likes chalk.

Eschscholtzia A member of the Poppy family, this is the Californian Poppy. It is an annual plant which is very easy to grow from seed sown in boxes in early spring, or sown out-of-doors in April. The plants should be set out one foot apart in May in well-dug soil.

Canterbury Bell This is a biennial plant which will do well in any well-dug soil. Sow the seed thinly out-of-doors in May, and set the plants out two feet apart in the autumn, when they will flower the following year. The plants need staking. Pick off the fading flowers and many more blooms will grow.

1 Delphinium 2 Gaillardia
3 Gypsophila 4 Eschscholtzia
5 Canterbury Bell

Allium A member of the Lily family. There are many varieties, all with beautiful flowers, but they all require a sunny position and well-drained soil, and do best on rockeries. The seed should be sown in a cold frame in spring.

Pink One of the real old-fashioned garden flowers which has never lost its popularity. The white variety, known as Mrs. Sinkins, is perhaps the best known. The seed should be sown out-of-doors in summer, but once the plants are established, they can be increased by pulling the young shoots out of the sockets of the old plants, and re-planting them in sandy soil out-of-doors in summer.

Saxifrage There is an enormous variety of Saxifrages. Some of them are very small and moss-like in their growth, while others are quite tall, loose and spreading. They are all hardy alpine plants, and most of them are very suitable for rockeries. It is best to plant in the autumn.

Lithospermum A dwarf, evergreen, creeping shrub which produces a wealth of bright blue flowers in early summer. It is particularly suitable for rockeries. It is sometimes known as Gromwell.

Armeria Commonly known as Thrift, this is a native British plant. There are a great many garden varieties, which are particularly suited to sunny positions in the rockery.

Gentian A hardy alpine plant which is best grown in rockeries or in old sinks. The one in the picture is called Acaulis, and it likes a gravel soil. Gentians are said to be difficult to grow, but this is because they are often planted in unsuitable soil.

1 Allium *2 Pink*
3 Saxifrage *4 Lithospermum*
5 Armeria *6 Gentian*

Lily The national flower of France. The ones in the picture are all out-door Lilies. *L. Auratum*, from Japan, likes plenty of leaf-mould and a certain amount of shade. The others all like the sun, but want their roots shaded, so it is a good thing to put them among other plants. *L. Regale*, from China, is easy to grow and reaches a height of six feet. *L. Martagon*, about three feet high, is also easy to grow and flowers freely. *L. Tigrinum*, the Tiger Lily, four feet high, flowers in September, which is later than the others. Lily bulbs should be planted in the autumn in holes filled with sand five inches deep and six inches apart. After flowering, do not cut the flower stems down until they are yellow.

Meconopsis A member of the Poppy family. The one in the picture is the famous Blue Poppy of Tibet. It is a very hardy perennial. Sow the seed in August, in soil with plenty of leaf-mould. *M. Cambrica*, the Welsh Poppy, has yellow flowers and is even hardier.

1 Lily
2 Meconopsis

Achillea A member of the Daisy family, often known as Yarrow. It is one of the easiest plants to grow, for it is hardy and does not mind what sort of soil it grows in. In fact, it will do well on heavy, cold ground. You can increase the plants by dividing them in autumn or spring.

Alstromeria The Peruvian Lily. Though hardy, it grows best in a sunny, sheltered position and prefers sandy soil. If you remove the flowers as soon as they fade you will get blooms practically throughout the summer. You can increase the plants by division in the autumn, but you should not do it every year.

Anchusa A hardy perennial which grows vigorously in cool moist places. It does not need a rich soil. Sow the seed in the spring for flowering the following year; or the plants can be increased by division in the autumn.

Helenium A member of the Daisy family and another very easy plant to grow, for it is hardy and will do well in any good garden soil, flowering in late summer. It is easy to grow from seed, and can also be increased by division in the spring.

1 *Achillea*
2 *Alstromeria*
3 *Anchusa*
4 *Helenium*

Kniphofia A member of the Lily family, commonly known as " Red-hot Poker ". Start by sowing seed in spring, but once the plants have grown, the roots can be divided in spring to get more plants. Kniphofia does best in rich soil. In the autumn the long leaves must be tied in knots, and let them wither before snapping them off.

Gladiolus A member of the Iris family. It is best to start by buying corms (bulbs), for the seeds take two years to flower. Plant the corms one foot apart in a sunny position, and put some sand and peat or leaf-mould in the holes. The plants must be staked. In November lift the corms and store them in a box of sand for use the following year.

Carnation A member of the Dianthus family. It is best to start with some of the border varieties, which are evergreens. Get young plants in spring and plant them one and a half feet apart in deeply-dug soil, putting some ashes in the holes. Each plant must be staked.

Lobelia The dwarf one shown in the picture is the best to start with, for it makes a wonderful edging for flower beds, and will bloom for several months. Sow the seed in a frame in the winter. Once you have plants you can increase them by taking cuttings in the autumn, but you must grow the cuttings in pots.

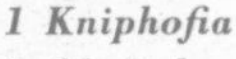

1 Kniphofia
2 Gladiolus
3 Carnation
4 Lobelia

Nasturtium Climbing Nasturtiums should be grown against a wall or on a pergola. The smaller varieties do well in ornamental urns, as shown in the picture, or at the front of flower borders. They are very easy to grow, but do not like rich soil. Sow the seed outside in spring to flower in the summer. When the plants appear, thin them to nine inches apart.

Hollyhock There are perennial and annual Hollyhocks. It is best to start with the annual varieties. Sow the seeds under glass towards the end of winter, and set the plants out in June, when they will flower in July or August. They need staking, and do especially well against a fence or wall.

Geranium The plants shown in the picture are called Pelargoniums. They can only be grown in pots. Geraniums can be taken from their pots in June and set out in the flower borders, but really these are greenhouse plants, and they cannot be grown successfully without a greenhouse.

Antirrhinum A native British plant, commonly called " Snapdragon ". Sow the seed under glass in March. When the baby plants appear, prick them out three inches apart and allow them plenty of air. Set them out in May one foot apart and they will flower before midsummer.

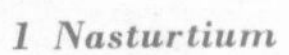

1 Nasturtium
2 Hollyhock
3 Geranium
4 Antirrhinum

Echinops This is the Globe Thistle, a hardy perennial plant which grows about three feet high and blooms in the summer. It is very easy to grow in any ordinary garden soil, and the plants can be increased by dividing the roots in spring.

Anemone Japonica A member of the Buttercup family. The variety shown in the picture blooms in late summer and autumn. To start with, a plant must be bought, but after that the only difficulty is keeping it within bounds. It spreads very rapidly and, if the plant is not kept under strict control, will soon swamp other plants and even force its way up through gravel paths.

Coleus This is an evergreen shrub which is valued for its coloured leaves, the flowers being quite insignificant. Though Coleus can be put out in the border for the summer, as shown in the picture, they are really greenhouse or conservatory plants, and cannot be kept through the winter unless the plants are potted-up and placed in a warm greenhouse.

Begonia This is another plant which cannot really be managed without a greenhouse, for it must be grown in a pot in heat until May. Begonias can then be planted out in June, in rich soil, in a fairly shady position. After flowering they must be lifted in September, and the tubers (which correspond to bulbs) stored in a dry place for the winter, potting them up again in the spring.

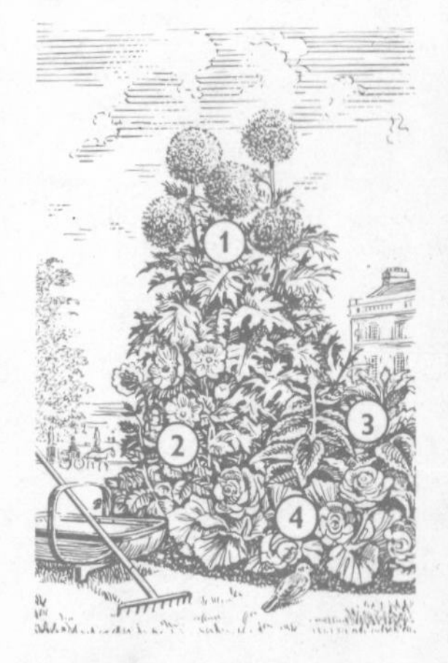

1 Echinops
2 Anemone Japonica
3 Coleus
4 Begonia

Clematis A member of the Buttercup family. Clematis are beautiful climbing plants, which can be grown up walls or over a trellis or a tree stump. They need good, rich soil with plenty of manure, and a sunny position. They are best planted in autumn and should be given plenty of water in the spring.

Climbing Rose The true Climbing and Rambler Roses are Polyantha Roses, which grow vigorously and bear abundant clusters of single or double flowers. They are excellent for growing up pillars, over arches, or against walls. They need scarcely any pruning, but the dead flowers should always be removed.

Passion Flower A beautiful climber which blooms in summer, not really hardy and must be planted in a sheltered position. A good idea is to cut back the side shoots to one inch from the base in February. The plant gets its name because the various parts resemble the articles used at the crucifixion of Christ. The leaf is the spear; the tendrils, the scourges; the column, the pillar of the Cross; the anthers, the hammer; the styles, the nails. The white signifies purity and the blue, heaven.

Ipomoea A member of the Convolvulus family, commonly known as "Morning Glory". The best are the annuals, which are easily grown from seed. Sow the seed in a frame in spring and plant out, using plenty of sand, for summer flowering.

1 Clematis
2 Climbing Rose
3 Passion Flower
4 Ipomoea

Pelargonium The one shown in the picture is the Ivy-leaved Pelargonium. Like the Geranium described on page 32, it can only be grown in a pot (when it must be trained up stakes) or in a hanging basket. The basket may be put out-of-doors from June to September, but must be brought in for the winter.

Agapanthus This is the African Lily from the Cape of Good Hope. It is not hardy and so is best grown in a large tub, so that it can be moved indoors for the winter. You can get more plants by division in spring.

Amaryllis Belladonna The Belladonna Lily. Another tub plant which may be placed out-of-doors in a sheltered position in September, but must be brought in for the winter. The bulbs should be planted in a compost of three parts loam to one part leaf-mould and one quarter part sand. The leaves come after the beautiful flowers.

Carpentaria An evergreen shrub which grows to ten feet high and bears scented flowers in June. Any garden soil suits it, but it must have the shelter of a wall, if it is to survive the winter.

Petunia A member of the Potato family. It is an annual, which likes a sunny position and bears a profusion of brilliant flowers. Any soil will do, but it must be kept well-watered. The dead heads should be picked off to encourage further flowering. It is best to buy plants (which are cheap) and to set them one foot apart.

1 Pelargonium 2 Agapanthus
3 Amaryllis Belladonna
4 Carpentaria 5 Petunia

Foxglove This is a biennial, which means that you should sow the seed one year to give flowering plants the next. But, as a matter of fact, once you have got Foxgloves you need not bother to sow seed, because they seed themselves freely, and you will find them popping up all over the place.

Periwinkle This is a hardy evergreen, which is valuable in the garden because it will grow under trees and in other shady places where most plants will not grow. Moreover, it is not a bit particular about the sort of soil. You can get more plants by division in the spring.

Solomon's Seal This is another plant which likes shady places, but it will not grow actually under trees. It is wonderfully graceful and very hardy, but is slow growing. It is best planted in the autumn.

St. John's Wort There are many varieties of this hardy perennial. One of the most popular is sometimes known as the " Rose of Sharon ". It will grow almost anywhere (even under trees) and is practically evergreen. It should be planted one foot apart in the autumn, and it will then form a dense mass.

1 Foxglove
2 Periwinkle
3 Solomon's Seal
4 St. John's Wort

Sunflower A member of the Daisy family. The one shown in the picture is the Common Sunflower, which is a hardy annual, growing to a height of six to ten feet. It is easily grown from seeds sown one quarter of an inch deep in ordinary soil, in a sunny position, where desired to flower.

Phlox One of the most magnificent perennial garden plants. It will thrive in any good soil, but needs plenty of watering. Phloxes are easy to grow from seed sown in frames in summer, and the plants can be increased by division at any time between November and April.

Michaelmas Daisy There is an enormous variety of Michaelmas Daisies in many different colours and heights. All are hardy perennials and flower when most other garden plants are past their best. They are easy to grow in almost any soil, and can be increased by division in spring just when they begin to grow. Plants which have stood for two years should always be divided.

Montbretia A South African plant which does well in sunny borders in well-drained soil. Plant the bulbs three inches deep and two inches apart in March or April, with a little sand in the holes. There is nothing else required for propagation.

1 Sunflower
2 Phlox
3 Michaelmas Daisy
4. Montbretia

Chrysanthemum This is the " Golden Flower " of the Chinese. The perennial varieties are in bloom through the summer from May to October. The annual varieties are easy to grow from seed and flower in a few weeks. The annuals are especially good for indoor decoration. Both sorts will flourish in sunny positions in any good garden soil.

Zinnia Zinnias are annuals of most brilliant colours. They should be planted in June, and until they begin to grow should be sheltered from the wind. A bit of sacking will do this very well. They grow very fast, and must then be tied to a good stake or they will blow over.

Limonium Bonduelli A member of the Plumbago family. The one in the picture comes from Algeria and is an annual. It has to be grown in pots indoors (the seed should be sown in February) and then transplanted out-of-doors in May. It must have a sunny position.

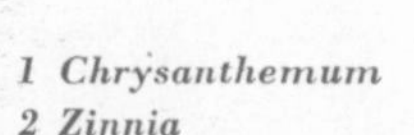
1 Chrysanthemum
2 Zinnia
3 Limonium Bonduelli

Golden Rod A member of the Daisy family. It will thrive in any soil and either in sun or shade. Sow the seed out-of-doors in April. The plants can be increased by splitting the roots in winter, but this will probably not be necessary, as Golden Rod often spreads so quickly that it becomes almost a weed.

Dahlia Another member of the Daisy family, which came originally from Mexico. There are a great many different sorts, but all require a deep, fertile and moist soil. All Dahlias, to flower properly, require a lot of watering during the growing stage. Dahlias can be grown from seed, but it is better to start by buying plants in the spring for delivery in June. The tubers (corresponding to bulbs in other plants) should be lifted in the autumn and stored for the winter in a dry, frost-proof place, for replanting the following year. If this is done, each plant will last for several years.

Helichrysum Another member of the Daisy family, commonly known as the " Everlasting Flower " The seeds should be sown in boxes in February, and the plants set out one-and-a-half feet apart in May. If the flowers are gathered early and hung head downwards in bunches in a cool, dry place, the colour will remain throughout the winter.

1 Golden Rod
2 Dahlia
3 Helichrysum

Philadelphus A member of the Saxifrage family. Often called Syringa or Mock Orange. This is a beautiful and very hardy shrub with a wonderful scent. It will thrive in any ordinary soil. After flowering all the old wood should be cut out.

Hibiscus A member of the Mallow family. The one in the picture is Syriacus, a hardy shrub which blooms late in summer and seems to do particularly well near towns. You can increase the plants by taking cuttings and planting them in sand, with leaf-mould, in a cold frame. They should be planted out in the autumn.

Hydrangea A member of the Saxifrage family. Because of their large heads of bloom, Hydrangeas are very popular as pot plants indoors, and many people think of them only as indoor plants. There are hardy outdoor ones as well, but, as a matter of fact, many of the pot plants will do perfectly well out-of-doors, if they are planted as soon as they have finished flowering.

1 Philadelphus
2 Hibiscus
3 Hydrangea

INDEX OF GARDEN FLOWERS

INDEX—continued